The Book of

Psalms

The Heart of the Word

FAMILY BIBLE STUDY GUIDE SERIES

The Book of

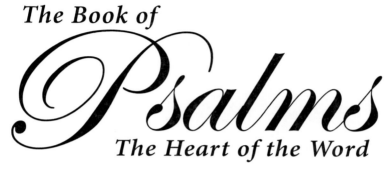

The Heart of the Word

Book v, Part ii: Psalms 120–150

Kevin Swanson

Generations

Published by:
Generations
19039 Plaza Drive Ste 210
Parker, Colorado 80134
www.generations.org

For more information on this and
other titles from Generations,
visit *www.generations.org* or call *888-389-9080.*

CONTENTS

INTRODUCTION

AN ENCOURAGEMENT TO FAMILY DEVOTION

"Let not thine heart envy sinners: but be thou in the fear of the LORD all the day long."
(Proverbs 23:17)

My encouragement to each Christian family that handles these devotionals, is to seek a family devotion that extends beyond a single experience of Bible reading and worship each day. While it is important to teach the Scriptures to our children, and to cultivate daily disciplines in the Word, there is more to Christian family life than that. We are looking for a family devotion, a fear of the Lord all the day long. The tenor of the Christian home is formed on the fear of God and is mixed with rejoicing and gratitude.

Every household in every culture around the world lives with a certain orientation that governs the general attitude, goals, priorities, and life of that household. This orientation is foundational to everything else. It is a fear, a reverence, and a worship for something or somebody. Most unbelieving households in our culture live in the fear, the reverence, and the worship of money and materials, power and popular opinion. Pagan households in times past lived in the fear of the spirits or the gods. It should not be difficult to trace the entire attitude of the home, along with its goals, priorities, and activities back to this one question: who or what do you fear? Who or what has got you in its grip?

For the Christian, the fear of God is the beginning of wisdom and knowledge—in everything. This includes knowledge concerning sin, salvation, and the death and resurrection of Christ. Without the fear of God, these things mean nothing to the mind of the natural man.

We could not possibly develop a biblical perspective of the family without this foundational consideration. When the psalms set out to describe the godly vision for family, this characteristic is mentioned first:

"Praise the Lord! Blessed is the man who fears the Lord, who delights greatly in His commandments. His descendants will be mighty on earth; the generation of the upright will be blessed." (Psalm 112:1, 2)

"Blessed is every one who fears the Lord, who walks in His ways. When you eat the labor of your hands, you shall be happy, and it shall be well with you. Your wife shall be like a fruitful vine in the very heart of your house, your children like olive plants all around your table. Behold, thus shall the man be blessed who fears the Lord." (Psalm 128:1-4)

The God-fearing household is the God-blessed household. This is where all the blessings begin. Naturally, this calls for faith that God really is a "rewarder of them that diligently seek Him." (Heb. 11:6) When my children reflect on their father, I want them to see a man who was always willing to put his entire fortune, his entire reputation, his ministries, and his position on the line for one politically-incorrect message— one unpopular stance that still accords with God's standard of righteousness. My father lost half of his support on the mission field when he suggested to his support base in the States that God was sovereign over every aspect of reality and truth. He wrote books on the sovereignty of God and six-day Creation—not exactly the most popular topics among Christian churches in the 1970s. He sincerely believed that this was God's truth, and for Dad, the fear of God trumped everything.

I believe this was the most defining moment in the life of my father's ministry (especially for his family). All six children have steadfastly maintained a strong allegiance to these doctrines, and continue to serve the Lord in various Christian churches around the world.

Popular opinion swings wildly from one extreme to another. Materials come and go. Churches are here today and gone tomorrow. Success is a slippery thing in this world. There is no more potent, more stabilizing, more defining, or more blessed contribution we can make to our children's lives, than to live before them in the fear of God all the day long, for thirty, forty, or fifty years.

The fear of the true and living God is the best fear of them all. It dispels all fear of circumstances, mitigating anxieties. It displaces any fear of relationships and codependency. We are more afraid of offending God, than we are of offending our children in the case that they need correction or restraint. This was where Eli went wrong with his sons, and consequently his family was subjected to the imprecation of God (1 Sam. 3:13). There is no down side to the fear of God in our homes. In fact, we are promised that this fear of God offers the best possible security for our children. The most stable households are the ones that fear God.

Let us also remember that this fear of God is the fear, love, honor, and reverence of a Father. We fear the "God and Father of our Lord Jesus Christ" (Eph. 1:3). It is no craven fear, for we know the Father if we have come to know the Son through the Gospel (John 14:7-9).

What This Fear Looks Like

One of the ways that we live out this fear before our children is by defending the Father's name. We react strongly against any irreverence towards the name of God (Exod. 20:7). In my growing up years, I remember that my father would carefully mark out minced oaths in some of our children's books. Whenever authors would use the word "gosh" for God, or "darn" for "damn," or "heck" for hell, my father recognized these words as God's sacred name and works. It is God's prerogative to damn things to hell, and the judgment of God ought never to be treated lightly. These are the little things that children never forget. When our Lord referred to the Father, He prayed to his "Holy Father" (John 17). In His instruction on praying, He has instructed us to "hallow" the name of our Father. Rushing through the name of God in our prayers, using the name in a thoughtless, repetitive, and reckless manner, ought to be avoided. Our children will mainly hear of the fear of God as it is patterned by their father or mother in prayer. Actually, over the years you will find that your children will generally pray in the same manner, using the same words and inflections that you have used over the years. Will they learn to fear God in your household?

"Come, you children, listen to me; I will teach you the fear of the Lord." (Psalm 34:11)

Thanksgiving

Before Paul launches into his admonitions concerning the family in Colossians 3, he carries out a line of thinking that is instructive for us to follow. He is speaking to Christians here, those who have been baptized into Christ. He says, "We have been raised with Christ, and we have died with Him, and our life is now hidden with Christ in God" (vs. 1-4). That is our new position. Henceforth, we are all empowered to put on tender mercies, kindness, humility, meekness, and longsuffering, providing forgiveness for each other all the day long (vs. 12). That is our new life in Christ. The words that summarize this new life from day to day are found in verses 16 and 17:

"Let the word of Christ dwell in you richly in all wisdom, teaching and admonishing one another in psalms and hymns and spiritual songs, singing with grace in your hearts to the Lord. And whatever you do in word or deed, do all in the name of the Lord Jesus, giving thanks to God the Father through Him." (Col. 3:16-17)

From here on out, it is a life of singing and gratitude! If the fear of God is the concrete in the foundation of the home, thanksgiving is the drywall, the furnishings, and the window coverings of the home! We thank the Lord for one another, precious souls loved by Christ and saved by His blood. We experience a perpetual relief from sins forgiven, joy of divine reconciliation, and an acceptance into the family of God. We are thankful for each blessing, each relationship, all evidences of life (spiritual and physical), our eternal inheritance, God's majestic creation, the water, the sun, the air we breathe, physical protection, and every sign of His kingdom. In the darkest days, we thank the Lord for every glimmer of light and every evidence of His goodness.

Years ago, I was on a ministry trip with with one of my daughters, and I was particularly concerned for her spiritual life at that time. Waking up at 3:00 in the morning, I lay in bed in anguish of spirit and poured out my petitions to God for her. It was at that moment that she murmured the name of Jesus in her sleep, and I was instantly comforted. That was all I needed for encouragement at that moment, and I thanked the Lord for it - a glimmer of light, a cloud the size of man's hand. We thank God for the smallest blessings at every opportunity.

The Basic Elements of Family Devotion

"It is the Spirit who gives life; the flesh profits nothing. The words that I speak to you are spirit, and they are life. . . From that time many of His disciples went back and walked with Him no more. Then Jesus said to the twelve, "Do you also want to go away?" But Simon Peter answered Him, "Lord, to whom shall we go? You have the words of eternal life." (John 6:63-69)

The Word of God is the very lifeblood of the family. It is our food and drink, and we cannot survive without it. Until the family (and the husband and wife especially) sees the vital necessity of the ministry of the Word, there will be spiritually emaciated and hardened souls sitting around the living room. I would not want to impose any minimum time requirement, but I would recommend a consistent, daily regimen. This is the thrust of Hebrews 3:13. Fifteen minutes of daily time in the Word is better than an inconsistent hour-long convocation once or twice a week.

Several years ago, I asked my father if he had been discipled by his father. His response surprised me. He told me that his father had read the Bible faithfully to his family, but he didn't have a relationship with his father. Although traditional Christianity in the 1940s and 1950s typically maintained respect for the Scriptures, there was something stilted about the communication of God's Word in homes at that time. In some homes, the family Bible appeared prominently on the coffee table in the living room but it was never opened. Thankfully, there was still something of a viable heritage of faith in my family background.

However, the Word is meant to come alive. It is meant to be relevant to every situation. It is interesting that Ephesians 6:4 and Hebrews 13:3 does not simply instruct us to "read the Word." That is not the biblical imperative. We are called to come along side and encourage each other through exhortations. We are to apply the Word to the relevant needs of present situations. Given that we have been in relationship and in communication with one another in the home, we should be able to make relevant applications.

Let's make this as simple as possible. We take up the Word and find an admonition in the Proverbs such as, "Go to the ant, you sluggard. Consider her ways and be wise." And so, we speak of the problem of slothfulness and how it affects our physical and spiritual life. We point out the work of Christ, who gave Himself for us in order that we might not henceforth live for ourselves but live for Him (2 Cor. 5:14). Then, we use the example of the diligent little ants. We note that these little creatures do not need a supervisor micro-managing their every activity. Nobody is telling the little ant to make his bed or do his school work. The ants appear to be self-motivated. Then, we think about ourselves. "Yesterday," you might say, "I noticed the kitchen waste basket was filled clear to the brim, and banana peels were falling on to the floor... and I saw nobody take the initiative to empty it. I think we may have a problem with laziness in our family. This may be a problem with all of us, myself included." Then, you take a moment to confess this sin and ask for God's forgiveness in and through Jesus Christ. That is how to take relevant Scripture and apply it to your particular family's situation. This cannot be done by a Sunday School teacher or a pastor who sees the child for only thirty minutes each week. It is the parent who lives with the child who is best fitted to provide that personal discipleship.

Briefly, here is a summary of the most important elements of family discipleship.

1. Read the Bible and draw out an exhortation. There are two words used in the New Testament that are translated "exhortation." The first word, *parakaleo,* is used in Hebrews 3:13 and Hebrews 10:25, and it is to use the Word of God to come alongside somebody else so as to encourage them in their Christian walk. It can involve a call to repentance, or a call to duty (Acts 2:40). The second word is *noutheteo*; this word is more direct and is sometimes translated "admonishment." This is the word used for exhorting children in Ephesians 6:4. (The word is also used for correcting the slothful in 1 Thess 5:14 and 2 Thess. 3:14).

2. Integrate Bible teaching into your daily routines as you sit in the house, as you walk by the way, as you rise up, and as you lie down. Your teaching is extemporaneous at many points only because the situation throughout the day changes so rapidly. Should you notice a billboard on the highway sporting the Proverbs 7 woman (immodest and sensuously presented), why not turn that into a teaching opportunity using the Word? "Son, there's the Proverbs 7 woman. We don't want to have fellowship with the unfruitful works of darkness, but we should rather reprove them." This integration of biblical truth into life should come naturally, regularly, and relevantly to the situation that confronts us.

3. Encourage discussion and questions. Biblical discipleship is usually described in terms of these back and forth interac-

tions (Exod. 12:26, 27; 13:14; Deut. 6:20-25), something that my father found missing in his relationship with his father, though he was raised in a Christian home. If this is missing in a discipleship experience, it is time to reexamine the quality of the relationships.

4. Catechisms can also be a good way to teach biblical truths. This is less extemporaneous and more formal. It should not displace the informal, or turn the discipleship into something more stilted and irrelevant to life. Nonetheless, Deuteronomy 6:7-9 commends both this formal teaching (where the Word is written on the posts and gates), and the informal, extemporaneous teaching as we "walk by the way."

The benefit of catechisms such as the Westminster Shorter Catechism is that they provide a comprehensive summary of the teachings of God's Word. We do not want our children leaving the home with giant gaps in their understanding of biblical truth, where they are subject to "every wind of doctrine and the cunning craftiness whereby men lay in wait to deceive" (Eph. 4:14). Most cults today grow by "evangelizing" children who were raised in Christian homes but were not grounded in biblical truth.

Before our children leave the home, they should be familiar with the basic theological truths presented in the Word, as well as the territories of mystery, and the clear boundaries of heresy. To provide just a few examples of these essentials:

- The doctrines of the Trinity and the Two Natures of Christ (and the mysteries that we do not understand)
- The nature of justification and sanctification, and how they relate
- The relationship of God's sovereignty and man's free will (and the mysteries that we do not understand)
- The right and wrong uses of the law of God
- The laws of God as laid out for the individual, family, church, and state

- The covenants of the promise, and how the Gentiles have access to these covenants

- The nature of the church as an organic body, an olive tree, a candlestick, and a vine

- The mysteries of the sacraments of Baptism and the Lord's Supper (and how to handle these mysteries with humility and care)

- The work of Christ and what it accomplished

- The work of the Holy Spirit and what it accomplishes

- The problems with the major heretical worldviews of humanism, relativism, eastern mysticism, Islam, and the cults

5. Teach the whole Word. I recommend reading for distance as well as depth. Our children need to know the entire story of God's covenant people from Old Testament into the New Testament. They should be familiar with the themes in every book of the Bible.

6. Bring other teachers into your home. When I speak of other teachers, I mean the great pastors and teachers with which the church has been blessed over the last two thousand years (Eph. 4:11). These are gifts to the church and we all should avail ourselves of them via books or recordings. During family gatherings, we have read books like Augustine's *Confessions*, John Bunyan's *Pilgrim's Progress*, *Grace Abounding to the Chief of Sinners*, *Foxe's Book of Martyrs*, Eusebius' *Ecclesiastical History*, and books written by the Puritans.

7. Focus on several key books of the Bible. Since it is practically impossible to train our children to be seminary theologians and experts on all 66 books of the Bible in 18 years, there is some wisdom in focusing on several key books.

- Focus on the Book of Genesis as providing a framework for history and God's dealings with man. This important book of the Bible sets the Christian perspective apart from the rest of the worldviews in the world in regards to origins, science, sociology, anthropology, history, and redemption.

- Focus on the Book of Proverbs as God's Book on Life, specifically designed for training young men and women in knowledge, wisdom, and understanding (Prov. 1:1-6). If we gave our children a great education in everything else, but forgot God's book of wisdom intended for the education of our children, we would be very poor parents indeed.

- Focus on the Book of Psalms as God's Book on Worship and Spiritual Battle. It is the very life-blood of the Christian who faces spiritual struggles. Christ had the Psalms on His lips at the cross, and the words of the Psalms should be written on the hearts of our children. They should know the basic content of every one of the 150 psalms by the time they leave the home. Granted, this is a tall order. If we see that God's Word is of higher value than every other book in the world, then we will spend a few hours in it every day.

- Focus on at least one Gospel—Matthew, Mark, Luke, or John. Your children should be very familiar with every one of these "pericopes" of the life of our Lord Jesus Christ, the very Son of God who came to save His people from their sins. As far as the teachings of Christ goes, your children should know the content from beginning to end of at least one of the Gospels. These Gospels contain the story of salvation and the revelation of Jesus Christ, the Son of God. If we want our children to know Jesus and to know the Gospel, and to go to heaven, they should be very familiar with this revelation.

- Focus on at least one doctrinal epistle. I would recommend Ephesians or Romans. The theology contained in the Bible is not written out in the same way systematic theology is. Essential to the Bible's theology are the organic connections of the smaller parts to the whole, which is why the Apostles were constantly mapping out the whole system of redemption in a single paragraph of five to ten verses. Our children should have a comprehensive knowledge of at least one of the epistles, such that they can map out the system of doctrine taught by Peter or Paul.

As a core aspect of the Generations ministry, we have produced in-depth Family Bible Study Guides on these key books of the Bible.

8. Memorize Scripture in order that you might meditate upon it. This is the Psalm 1 lifestyle for the Christian.

"Blessed is the man who walks not in the counsel of the ungodly, nor stands in the path of sinners, nor sits in the seat of the scornful; but his delight is in the law of the Lord, and in His law he meditates day and night. He shall be like a tree planted by the rivers of water, that brings forth its fruit in its season, whose leaf also shall not wither, and whatever he does shall prosper." (Psalm 1:1-3)

Memorization for the sake of memorization does not do much good, but to memorize so as to saturate oneself in the truths of God's Word is of tremendous value. As we memorize the Word, we are much better prepared to draw it in to our conversations and sweeten our home with God's truth.

A good way to memorize a verse as a family is to recite it three times together. Then, each family member takes a turn at it without referring to the text. Should anybody make a mistake, a parent should correct it quickly so that the wrong recitation is not engrained in everybody's mind. Finally, we recite the whole verse again in unison.

9. Pray without ceasing (1 Thess. 5:17). An entire book could be given to the topic of family prayer. This is where we bare our hearts to God and bring out every thanksgiving, every petition, and every praise contained within us. Sometimes, we know there is something that needs to be confessed, and some petition that needs to be drawn out, but we cannot quite verbalize it. Our hearts are heavy, and we know that we are in desperate need of God's help. It is just that we can't quite put a finger on what the real issue at hand is. In this case, we must rely on the Holy Spirit of God to assist us. We may begin by praying the Word—a verse or a psalm with which we can identify. This is why it is important to know the Psalms and a

great deal of the Word.

Provide opportunity for the other members of the household to pray as well. After praying myself, I will offer a long pause for others to join in. When it is clear that all have prayed who have felt the need to pray, I will say a final "Amen."

The Christian home should be bathed in prayer, as we turn to the Lord throughout the day. Even our younger children can be encouraged to pray before meals. Our children should know instinctively where the family goes when there are concerns and anxieties that arise.

Some men find it most difficult to pray out loud with their wives. Could this indicate pride or a lack of sincerity when it comes to their religious faith? We are most forced to honesty when we are with those who know us the best.

I am especially thankful for my mother's prayers. She has been a prayer warrior for many years, and I am convinced that this is one of the chief graces of God that has sustained our family in the faith through the generations. For hours every day, she faithfully prays for her children and her grandchildren. I doubt that there has been an exception to that routine for decades.

Leading by Example

The spiritual temperature of the home is very much dependent upon parents, especially the father. If we as parents have failed to be moved by the Word of God, how can we expect our children to be impressed by it? Our comfort, our strength, our life, and our joy must come through the Word. When the Word becomes relevant and alive to us, then we have something with which to minister to others in our home.

Of all of the great missionary stories of the 19th Century, the most powerful and inspiring is that of John G. Paton. His autobiography was certainly influential to Christians over the last 150 years. His faith in the face of the forces of darkness and many threats to his life in the New Hebrides is legendary. His steadfastness to the mission, his love for the people on these islands, and his successes through much adversity is incomparable to anything you will find in the history of missions. As we read his powerful testimony, we want to know where this man came from. How did he get this vision? We find the answer in the first chapter of his autobiography:

"How much my father's prayers at this time impressed me I can never explain, nor could any stranger understand. When, on his knees and all of us kneeling around him in Family Worship, he poured out his whole soul with tears for the conversion of the Heathen world to the service of Jesus, and for every personal and domestic need, we all felt as if in the presence of the living Savior, and learned to know and love him as our Divine friend. As we rose from our knees, I used to look at the light on my father's face, and wish I were like him in spirit, hoping that, in answer to his prayers, I might be privileged and prepared to carry the blessed gospel to some portion of the heathen world."[1]

There in that rustic home in the highlands of Scotland, an impoverished, simple father (who made his living sewing socks), would gather his nine children around him each day for family worship. The family's priorities were clear, as Paton writes:

"None of us can remember any day ever passed unhallowed thus. No hurry for market, no rush of business, no arrival of friends or guests, no trouble or sorrow, no joy or excitement, ever prevented at least our kneeling around the family altar, while the high priest led our prayers to God, and offered himself and his children there."[2]

In the providence of God, the kingdom of Christ often develops through a multi-generational vision. This takes place whenever the heart of a father for Christ and His Kingdom turns to his son, and his son's heart turns to his father and receives it (Mal. 4:6). When, by the grace of God, fathers pass that vision on to their children through discipleship, the kingdom of God benefits and good things happen! As sons are

1. John G. Paton, *The Autobiography of the Pioneer Missionary to the New Hebrides* (Edinburgh: Banner of Truth, 2013).
2. Ibid, 370.

enabled to stand on the shoulders of their humble fathers, a generational leverage develops for the extension of the Gospel and the further discipleship of the nations. May Christ's kingdom come in our generation by this means!

PSALM 120

Category: *Ascent, Deliverance*
Occasion: *Ungodly Company*
Author: *Unknown*

....

¹ In my distress I cried unto the Lord, and He heard me.
² Deliver my soul, O Lord, from lying lips, and from a deceitful tongue.
³ What shall be given unto thee? or what shall be done unto thee, thou false tongue?
⁴ Sharp arrows of the mighty, with coals of juniper.
⁵ Woe is me, that I sojourn in Mesech, that I dwell in the tents of Kedar!
⁶ My soul hath long dwelt with him that hateth peace.
⁷ I am for peace: but when I speak, they are for war.

The Point:

When exiled into an ungodly community that is consumed in ceaseless strife, the godly man longs for peace and for Zion.

How do we feel in the recitation of this Psalm?

We are distressed by the lack of peace in the world. We are sick of it. Spouses can't get along, family feuds are common, churches split, and nations go to war with each other. Deceit creates false

impressions all the time. Trust dissipates and relationships are tenuous. When a man loves peace, he cannot tolerate the wars, schisms,
divisions, and strife around him. In this terrible world of unceasing
conflicts, we long for peace. We cry out for it. We pray for God's
peace in Christ.

What does this Psalm say?

Psalm 120 is the first in a series of 15 psalms that bear the inscrip-
tion "Song of Ascent." Most translators believe that these are songs
that God's people would sing as they ascended the hill into the city
of Jerusalem for worship. Remember, the children of Israel would
travel to Jerusalem three times every year to worship. Thus, these
psalms are to be sung on the way to worship. They prepare us for
worship.

Verses 1–4

What happens when you are deceived? Very terrible things can happen when somebody deceives a friend with a lie. If a friend told you
the ice in a lake was deep enough to hold your weight, you might
trust him and proceed to walk across the ice. Should he have mis-
led you about the thickness of the ice, the consequences could be
catastrophic. Truth matters, and this world is full of liars that cause
much destruction to human souls. How can you know which teachers lie and which ones tell the truth? What if the liar to truth-teller
ratio were a hundred to one? What would be the chances of the average person getting the truth? In our world, deceptions, cults, and
false teachings are everywhere. For that reason, your ultimate hope
of being saved out of this world of untruth is found in God. "Deliver
my soul, O Lord, from lying lips, and from a deceitful tongue!"

Wicked men are characterized by a lack of interest in the truth—the
truth about God, the truth about other people, and the truth about
themselves. They think of themselves as righteous, and they refuse to
define right and wrong by the laws of God. They suppress whatever
truth is available to them (Rom. 1:18). Then, they set out to deceive
others through powerful mediums such as television, film, recorded
music, and college classes. This is how billions of people are taken to
hell in the present day. What shall be done to the false tongue? God

will judge. This is the message of the fourth verse.

Verses 5-7

Now the psalmist presents his current situation as very far removed from Jerusalem (the place of God's dwelling). Kedar and Mesech lie well outside beyond the land of Canaan, way over in the land of Arabia or Asia Minor. It is a land where there is no interest in peace. The wars of the nations are incessant. Either men are focused on micro-wars (divorces, church splits, etc.), or they are busy fighting other nations in bloody wars. This is the hobby that consumes natural man in his fallen estate. True Christians, however, are not all that interested in war. Occasionally they may have to defend their homes from marauders, but this is not their primary interest. They seek a local church body that opposes the world, and seeks peace within the walls of the church. If a local church community descends into bitter, malicious infightings, and worldly pursuits, the godly will leave and look elsewhere for a body of believers who seek peace with God and with each other.

When the believer is set among unbelievers, he finds himself in the tents of Kedar. He is a stranger among these folk, and he knows it and they know it. His one desire is always to return to the fellowship of the saints wherever it is to be found.

How do we apply this Psalm to our lives?

Peacemaking is a mark of a true church. If a church has no spirit of forgiveness, confession, and humility, it is not a church of Jesus Christ. However, the ministry of reconciliation is a gift that comes through Christ. Reconciliation is the business of the local church. First it is reconciliation with God, and then it is reconciliation with our brothers and sisters.

When a Christian brother works in the unbelieving world, he greatly desires the company of the saints and the worship of God. He feels like a fish out of water, or a bird far away from his nest. Even if he is pressed into the wars of the nations, his desire is still for peace. Even if he is a member of the national armed forces, every man in his battalion recognizes him as a true peacemaker (one who is always working to eliminate conflicts within his group, and to bring people to Christ).

How does this Psalm teach us to worship God?

The church is a place of peace. If there are ill-spirits between members of the congregation, we leave our gifts at the altar and repair relationships before entering into worship. We seek forgiveness and reconciliation, because we are in the fellowship of the forgiven. The Christian church offers the very best basis for unity available on earth. We are all great sinners, saved by the same great Savior! How can we worship the same Christ if we are at war with each other?

Questions:

1. What is the context of this psalm? Where are Mesech and Kedar?

2. What is the problem with deception?

3. What are the two things that mark the ungodly, as noted in this psalm?

4. How does the believer look at strife and war?

5. What is an Ascent Psalm? Which Psalms are categorized as Ascent Psalms?

Family Discussion Questions:

1. Should Christians fight in the military? Provide biblical justification.

2. Are we peacemakers or peace breakers? What does a peacemaker look like? What does a peace breaker look like?

PSALM 121

Category: Ascent, *Faith*
Occasion: *Threats to Safety*
Author: *Unknown*

....

1   I will lift up mine eyes unto the hills, from whence cometh my help.
2   My help cometh from the Lord, which made heaven and earth.
3   He will not suffer thy foot to be moved: He that keepeth thee will not slumber.
4   Behold, He that keepeth Israel shall neither slumber nor sleep.
5   The Lord is thy keeper: the Lord is thy shade upon thy right hand.
6   The sun shall not smite thee by day, nor the moon by night.
7   The Lord shall preserve thee from all evil: He shall preserve thy soul.
8   The Lord shall preserve thy going out and thy coming in from this time forth, and even for evermore.

The Point:

When our safety and well-being is threatened, we look to the Lord for our constant protection and preservation.

How do we feel in the recitation of this Psalm?

This could be one of the most comforting psalms in the Bible, along with Psalms 23 and 91. Throughout our lives we are constantly faced with treacherous conditions, not the least of which is the threat of physical harm and death. We climb on dangerous cliffs, covered with ice or loose gravel. Yet, we are confident in God's protection. We look up at the majestic Rocky Mountains, and we know that the Creator of these mountains will preserve us. The Creator of the mighty sun and moon will see to it that we are treated well by the sun and the moon and all of His creation.

As you read these words, as you hear these words, tighten your grip on the truths they represent. Replace the word "thee" with "me." Recite these words out loud if necessary, "The Lord is my keeper. The Lord is my shade upon my right hand. The sun shall not smite me by day."

What does this Psalm say?

Verse 1-2

On February 10, 2011, *Time* magazine published an article suggesting that, given the ongoing advancement of biogenetic technology, man would be immortal by the year 2045.

Where a man looks for salvation is an indication of his faith. More than ever, man is looking to himself for salvation from death and other physical enemies. But modern man is too confident in himself. The average life expectancy today (which is 71-79 years of age), is not much different from Moses' estimate in Psalm 90. Eventually, man will disappoint himself and prove to be a poor savior.

We must look beyond our circumstances, beyond the immediate concerns, beyond the enemies that surround us. This is what it means to lift our eyes to the hills. If we could just lift up our eyes to hills and to the heavens beyond, we would catch a glimpse of the powerful God who created all of this vast universe. Too often we are just shortsighted. All we can see are the immediate trials that confront us. We cannot see tomorrow, or the day after tomorrow, or into eternity. So as we study our circumstances, this becomes the sum total of our thoughts and we are quickly discouraged and distressed. That is when we need to look up and consider God who holds eternity in His hands, not to mention every single tomorrow that will ever come.

Where else would you put your confidence? Only the God who created heaven and earth can control all of the elements within the universe to save us physically and spiritually.

Verses 3-5

These are the "keeping" verses of this psalm: the word "keep" is used in each verse. The word connotes a guard who watches over an army camp during the night hours. God does not slumber in His careful watch over you and me. Though we may be tempted to think that He has forgotten about us on occasion, faith demands that we receive these words. Your life is in His hands. He is watching your every step, that you will not slip a single inch. This is very impressive imagery. God is arranging the rocks and the sand under your feet, such that you will not slide off the cliff of life.

In the spiritual sense, we are not always "on our game." This can be deadly, as we are truly in a dangerous battle (1 Tim. 1:19, Eph. 6:12ff). When the bullets are flying this way and that, only one who is 100% on his game will survive, and even then he would have to be "Superman" to guarantee his survival. A thousand things can go wrong. We grow weary. We lower our defenses. We struggle to stay awake in the battle, let alone develop adequate strategies to face off with the enemy. Thankfully, God does not slumber or sleep. He is infinitely capable of preserving us in the conflict.

"The Lord is your keeper." The wording presents to us the picture of a personal bodyguard. It is one thing to be sleeping in the barracks with a single guard watching from a guard tower above the camp. It is another thing to have the God of heaven constantly beside us, personally providing protection for us. Do you find comfort from these words?

Verses 6-8

From the vantage point of the earth, the sun and the moon are the most intimidating proximate objects in our solar system. No earthly power, no international governing force, no nuclear bomb, nothing could possibly save us if the sun should tumble into the earth.

In fact, there is no natural power in the whole universe that could save us from such a horrible predicament. God, on the other hand, can keep the sun in its place by a nudge of His little finger. While we may be subjected to endure a little evil here and there, we must see that God can turn the evil to good for us (Rom 8:28). Joseph experienced all sorts of evil intentions on the part of his brothers, Potiphar's wife, and others, but at the end, he testified that "God meant it for good" (Gen. 50:20). In effect, God had protected him from all evil. Shortly before he was executed, the Apostle Paul testified that God had delivered him from all evil (2 Tim. 4:17,18). He knew that his own martyrdom would only perfect his witness to the Roman world as an Apostle of Christ (2 Tim. 4:17). Martyrdoms only exponentially increase a man's total life impact for Christ, and these glorious deaths are immediately followed up by a glorious resurrection. As Christians we do need to see evil as real and present. It is true that evil will "try to get at us." But God will thwart all of these attempts. What tremendous comfort the believer can receive from these words!

How do we apply this Psalm to our lives?

We need to believe these words and act on them. When confronted by evil, we must not assume the worst outcome or even contemplate the worst. If we experience demonic attacks on our families, and our children exhibit rebellion, we must rather hope in the mercy of God. The man of faith says, "God can work through this. God will preserve us from all evil. He will work all things for good." Believing will only come by taking God on His Word.

We will take more risks if we hold to these truths. We will risk our lives for the sake of Christ. The missionary John Paton was surrounded by natives intending to destroy him on the island of Tanna. He writes later, "I could see the Lord Jesus Christ surveying all the scene. I knew that not a musket would fire, not a killing stone will be thrown without the permission of the Lord Jesus."

How does this Psalm teach us to worship God?

Every week that we "ascend" to our local church to worship God, we should thank the Lord for His protection over the previous week. Meditate on the tender love that Christ has for His church, especially since He has died for that church. This thought will frame our whole perspective of the church where we gather to worship.

Questions:

1. What is an "Ascent" Psalm?

2. What are some of the other comforting psalms of faith?

3. Why can't man save himself?

4. What are the biggest physical threats to life on earth?

5. What does the word "keep" mean, when we say that God "keeps" His people?

6. How did God protect Joseph and the Apostle Paul from evil despite the persecuting forces of evil?

Family Discussion Questions:

1. How secure do you feel in the love of God? When was the last time you felt great fear, anxiety, or insecurity? How did it resolve?

Psalm 122

Category: Ascent, *Thanksgiving*
Occasion: *Sunday Morning*
Author: *David*

....

¹ I was glad when they said unto me, Let us go into the house of the Lord.

² Our feet shall stand within thy gates, O Jerusalem.

³ Jerusalem is builded as a city that is compact together:

⁴ Whither the tribes go up, the tribes of the Lord, unto the testimony of Israel, to give thanks unto the name of the Lord.

⁵ For there are set thrones of judgment, the thrones of the house of David.

⁶ Pray for the peace of Jerusalem: they shall prosper that love thee.

⁷ Peace be within thy walls, and prosperity within thy palaces.

⁸ For my brethren and companions' sakes, I will now say, Peace be within thee.

⁹ Because of the house of the Lord our God I will seek thy good.

The Point:

The church is admirable for its peace and judgment.

How do we feel in the recitation of this Psalm?

While some may dread going to church on Sunday morning, this is not the case with us. We are drawn to this place because it is a place where glad hearts thank God for His goodness. We are especially thankful for the church itself—an institution that is not going to disappear. We have confidence in Christ's ability to build a church that cannot possibly be destroyed by the powers of hell or anything else.

What does this Psalm say?

Verses 1-3

This ascent psalm speaks of the heart of the man who is heading towards Jerusalem. He is coming home. The military man who has been away from home for a few years knows what it means to come home. He returns to the place of his kin, to the place he belongs, to the place of his childhood, to the place where he is loved and to the people he loves. When the Word uses the term "house of the Lord," it refers to the place of the family of God, the home where God's family dwells. There is a difference between a house and a home. If our children think that they come to a building when they worship God, they are thinking wrongly about the church. They come to a family. A good church is like a good home. Everybody enjoys being there, especially if they are members of the family of God.

Verse three speaks of the unity of the church and the solidarity of the body. Suppose you should come upon a human body where the legs and hands and kidneys were lying around in different places. Of course, you would be concerned about the integrity and the health of this body. When God puts a house together, there is integrity to it. This is one way to identify the church of God. It is held together not be sheer force and powerful dictators: it is held together by love.

Verses 4-5

These verses give a little more insight into what happens at this place called "Jerusalem." Here they find the "testimony of Israel." At the very center of the city and the temple, the children of Israel (and especially the priests) would see the "holiest of holies." In the center of this place, they would find the ark of the covenant. Inside the ark, they would discover the tables of the law, which is the testimony of God Himself to His people. Wherever God's people gather, they should find the Word of God at the very core of it. They will not find altars, candles, pictures, images, food, or even communion tables. They will find men telling and hearing the words of God.

Second, there is thanksgiving in this place. Where God's people gather, they are sensitive to the good things that God has done to them. Despite the many trials and difficulties, they can still say that God has been kind to them through it all. He has bound up their wounds. He has healed their spiritual diseases. He has purged away the guilt and corruption of their sin.

Third, Jerusalem is a place of judgment. There are two things that make this world a terrible place—immorality and conflict. When God redeems a people, He solves both problems. Thus, the people of God will always be characterized by righteousness and peace. The church will be markedly different from society around them, and this will be clear by the standards of judgment. In the city of God, men and women are purified by the blood of Christ and by faith in Christ, There is cleansing going on, and Paul can say this of the church in 1 Corinthians 6:9-11:

"Do you not know that the unrighteous will not inherit the kingdom of God? Do not be deceived. Neither fornicators, nor idolaters, nor adulterers, nor homosexuals, nor sodomites, nor thieves, nor covetous, nor drunkards, nor revilers, nor extortioners will inherit the kingdom of God. And such were some of you. But you were washed, but you were sanctified, but you were justified in the name of the Lord Jesus and by the Spirit of our God."

Meanwhile, the cities of the heathen think nothing of convenience divorce, adultery, and habitual drunkenness—these are sins that warrant discipline within the church. Therefore, everybody walking into Jerusalem knows that, within the church, order replaces chaos. Those who walk disorderly are marked and firmly corrected—and sometimes removed from the fellowship (2 Thess. 3:6). These "thrones of judgment" bear the sword of the Word and the spiritual keys of the kingdom. Even in nations where God's law is repudiated by the civil magistrate, there are faithful churches wherein righteousness prevails and good judgment is maintained. This should be comforting to every soul that hungers and thirsts after righteousness.

Verses 6–9

The remainder of this psalm focuses on a familiar element of the ascent psalms. Peace must also characterize the church of Jesus Christ. It is essential. Every elder and deacon in the church of Christ must be relentlessly, doggedly pursuing peace. No quarrelsome man belongs in church leadership, not in the city of peace. David here encourages us to pray for peace, to desire peace, and to pursue it with all our hearts.

When peace is shattered in a local church, or when denominations pull apart, the consequences are devastating. Relationships are destroyed. Hearts are crushed and embittered. Apostasy is usually present on all sides. Peace is a blessing to our family members, our brothers and sisters, and our friends (verse 8). For the same reason that you do not want foreign nations bombing your cities and your homes, you do not want the peace destroyed in the body of your local church.

Given that the church is the family of God, all elders, pastors, and stewards of the "house" should handle the "household" affairs carefully. This is a very special family, and God Himself has put much careful work into this house. Since it is the house of God, all of us should seek the good of the house.

How do we apply this Psalm to our lives?

Let us do all in our power to seek the peace of the church. As the passage puts it, those who love the church will prosper. Those families that are addicted to the ministry of the saints will flourish.

How does this Psalm teach us to worship God?

We come to the church to offer our sacrifices of thanksgiving. Let us not forget that the core of worship is thanksgiving (verse 4). It is praising God and thanking Him for what He has done for us. If we never quite make it to thanksgiving in all of our teaching and petitions and prayers, we haven't quite made it into worship.

Questions:

1. What is the house of the Lord?

2. What are the characteristics that mark out Jerusalem (or the church) in this psalm?

3. What would the Israelites find at the very center of the holiest of holies in their worship?

4. What is a chief characteristic of an elder or leader in the church?

5. Provide several examples of Thanksgiving Psalms.

Family Discussion Questions:

1. Does our family love the church? How is this evident in our lives?

PSALM 123

Category: *Ascent, Deliverance*
Occasion: *Corporate Affliction*
Author: *Unknown*

....

1   Unto thee lift I up mine eyes, O thou that dwellest in the heavens.
2   Behold, as the eyes of servants look unto the hand of their masters, and as the eyes of a maiden unto the hand of her mistress; so our eyes wait upon the Lord our God, until that He have mercy upon us.
3   Have mercy upon us, O Lord, have mercy upon us: for we are exceedingly filled with contempt.
4   Our soul is exceedingly filled with the scorning of those that are at ease, and with the contempt of the proud.

The Point:

In an extremely weakened state, a beaten-down church cries out to God for His mercy upon them.

How do we feel in the recitation of this Psalm?

We are mocked, criticized, castigated, and humiliated, and we are powerless to remedy our condition. We may be persecuted by powerful governments, marginalized by major media sources, or shamed by the academic elites. They point out our weaknesses and our hypocrisies, while celebrating their own high immoralities. All we can do is look to God for His eventual vindication and restoration.

What does this Psalm say?

Verses 1-2

Many of us do not know what it is like to be subjected to abject poverty or chattel servitude. We have sufficient food in the cupboards, and savings accounts to cover a rainy day. If we find one employer too severe, we can always find another one. We can do contractual work on the side, or start an entrepreneurial venture on a part time basis. The psalmist speaks here of the man locked into perpetual servitude, not having a dime to his name or any possibility of emancipation. Whatever food he gets is limited to what the master gives him. He cannot escape. He cannot steal from his master, or he will be severely chastised. He is utterly dependent upon his master for whatever food he receives. This is the analogy used by the psalmist in these verses. We look up to God for mercy, as a slave looks to his master for food. As the slave's only hope for survival is found in the generosity of the master, so we look to God for His vindication and salvation.

This psalm expresses a need for mercy. Helpless people need mercy. We therefore turn to God who is full of mercy and ready to show mercy, and ask Him for this mercy. It is only the people who do not see themselves as helpless and needy of mercy that do not receive mercy.

Verses 3-4

The condition of God's people (and the church) is revealed in these verses. We have seen the church disintegrate into denominational fragments, each of which becomes successively liberal generation by generation. Internal conflicts tear at the heart of local churches. Leaders appear incapable of discerning between majors and minors, gnats and camels. The "most conservative" churches are devastated by scandals, and the mainstream media gleefully records the explicit details on the news. The younger generation, overcome by cynicism, walk away from the church. And the rest who are left standing in the cold empty buildings wrestle with doubts and faithlessness themselves. The discouragement is stifling. The shame and suffering is unrelenting. We have nowhere else to look, but to the Christ who initiated this project of the church.

God's people are scorned by those that sit at ease (verse 4). Generally, it is those who are unconcerned about their sin that appear to be so much better off than those poor souls who are tormented by tempters, convicted by the conscience, and severely taxed in a war with the flesh. The pseudo-Christians cruise along on the Celestial railroad, mocking the pilgrims struggling along the pathway towards heaven. Why do those pilgrims make such a big ordeal out of sin? It would be so much easier to ignore the sin, teach forgiveness of sins without repentance, and be done with it.

The Christian life introduces to us painful spiritual realities and drives us to a bloody cross again and again. It forces us to our knees to cry out with the publican, "God have mercy on me, a sinner!" This scene does not look impressive to the world. In fact, the world will just mock at it. But we will continue extending our hands up to the heavens, begging for mercy from the only One who can give it to us.

How do we apply this Psalm to our lives?

If you have never seen yourself in this state of helplessness and humiliation, marginalized and crying out for mercy, you don't know what it is to be part of the people of God. Of course, there are times when we enjoy the sense of progress, success, and serenity in the church, but there are other times when we see ourselves as the remnant, badly persecuted and afflicted. Both elements have a measure of truth to them. In contrast with the powers of the world around us, the church appears diminutive and weak. Like a tiny rubber raft in hurricane-wracked waves three hundred feet high, the church barely stays afloat. The great empires of men appear to us like gigantic aircraft carriers in contrast, but they are crushed to pieces by these same winds and waters. It is only God's miraculous preservation that keeps this little rubber raft bobbing along in the waters.

How does this Psalm teach us to worship God?

Worship leaders must maintain a sharp self-awareness of the weakness of God's people. Regardless of the size of the church building, budget, or attendance, we cannot forget the vulnerability of the body. "We are weak, but He is strong. We need His mercy." This is the message that returns again and again in the corporate worship of the church.

Questions:

1. What can a slave do to obtain his food? How does this form a picture of our relationship to God?

2. Who are the people that scorn at believers?

3. Why do believers sometimes seem so downcast, while unbelievers appear to be at ease?

4. Which series of psalms are known as the Ascent Psalms?

5. Give several examples of Deliverance Psalms.

Family Discussion Questions:

1. How do we see the church of Christ with which we fellowship (our local church or denomination)? Is it weak or strong? Is it getting weaker or getting stronger?

2. Who are the people that mock at the church of Christ today?

Psalm 124

Category: *Ascent, Faith*
Occasion: *Narrow Escape*
Author: *Unknown*

....

1   If it had not been the Lord who was on our side, now may Israel
    say;
2   If it had not been the Lord who was on our side, when men rose
    up against us:
3   Then they had swallowed us up quick, when their wrath was
    kindled against us:
4   Then the waters had overwhelmed us, the stream had gone over
    our soul:
5   Then the proud waters had gone over our soul.
6   Blessed be the Lord, who hath not given us as a prey to their
    teeth.
7   Our soul is escaped as a bird out of the snare of the fowlers: the
    snare is broken, and we are escaped.
8   Our help is in the name of the Lord, who made heaven and earth

The Point:

When the anger and pride of powerful forces rise up against us, only
God can deliver us, and He has delivered us.

How do we feel in the recitation of this Psalm?

The wrath of man is a frightening thing. When proud and wrathful people rise up against us, there is no telling what they will do. They will not rest until they have destroyed us. Most intimidating of all are the demonic powers, who would drag us to hell with them if they could. But now, we have escaped the claws of this malicious force. As we look back, we feel incredible relief that we have made such a harrowing escape.

What does this Psalm say?

Verses 1–3

The repetition of the first line increases the sense of relief expressed by the rescued. Have you ever escaped very narrowly from imminent death or disaster? From the bottom of your heart, you know that only supernatural intervention saved you from certain destruction. Your escape cannot be attributed to some assignable human cause. Such an experience will stick to you for a lifetime. You will tell your children and grandchildren about the amazing work of God in your life.

In this case, the psalmist has faced the threats of proud and wrathful men who are bound and determined to destroy him. Think about how hard it would be if the mafia put a contract on your life. These powerful cartels form a tight, conspiratorial network of wicked men such that it seems nigh impossible to escape their grasp. If this malevolent coalition against us were broad enough to include most of the major media, Hollywood, Nashville, the civil government, and the education establishment, it would appear impossible for the church to survive. Their entire systems are built upon human pride and academic hubris. And, if there is one thing they know—they hate the Christians who stand opposed to their licentiousness, their feminism, and their evolutionary godlessness.

Verses 4–5

The church is so small. The enemy is so much larger, and so dedicated to the destruction of the church, it is a wonder that the enemy doesn't destroy the church in short order. How did the Christian church survive the persecutions of the gigantic Roman Empire?

How did the church survive Darwin, Freud, Marx, Dewey, and Margaret Sanger? What single Christian of the last century comes close to matching their power and influence over human societies the world over? The streams would have gone over our soul, had it not been for the Lord who was on our side! The only possible explanation for the survival of the church worldwide (especially over the last 75 years) is that the Lord is on our side.

Verses 6-8

The salvation referenced here may be either individual or corporate salvation. Because these are ascent psalms, it would be best to take this as the church. When the Reformation-era church emerged out of the corrupted malaise of Romanism in the 16th century, it was a harrowing escape. The devil did not take kindly to it. Political disturbances produced tens of thousands of martyrs amongst the Waldensians, the French Huguenots, and the Scottish Covenanters. How so many devout, godly men and women could be so cruelly drowned, dismembered, and burned at the stake in the name of Christ boggles the mind! It must have been the devil who set snares in the minds of powerful popes and princes. Nonetheless, the Reformation succeeded, nations were transformed, and the missionary movement took the Word of God around the globe in subsequent centuries.

Freedom for the church in Holland and England eventually came about through William the Silent and his posterity. It all began during a hunting excursion with the King of France. As the King conversed with young William, he happened to reveal the intentions of the European powers to wipe out every Protestant in the Netherlands. William was silent. Then and there, he committed himself with strong resolution to counter the King's plan. And that he did, over the subsequent twenty years. God uses these seemingly insignificant historical moments to bring about the preservation of His work.

Whatever persecution the church will face in the future, it must cling to these words: "Our help is in the Name of the Lord who made heaven and earth!" We must remember who it is that we worship. Who is this God? He made a universe of a trillion galaxies. He made the most powerful angels, including those who turned their power to evil purposes. If this be the source of our help, who shall we fear? Why should we be afraid?

How do we apply this Psalm to our lives?

Let us not be too proud, or too fearful, concerning the state of the church. Both of these all-too human responses are unacceptable for us. On the one hand, there are formidable enemies that tear at the church and strip back the work, yet on the other hand, we must continue to build the church in faith that God will go before us.

How does this Psalm teach us to worship God?

The church is a place where we recount the salvation stories, from the Red Sea to Calvary. We speak of the narrow escapes, individually and corporately, and give God the glory for what He has done in the past. We look forward with eager expectation to what He is going to do in the future.

Questions:

1. What is the sentiment of this psalm?

2. What are the things that the ungodly hate about the church of Christ?

3. How did the enemy respond to the Reformation?

4. How did God preserve the Reformation church?

5. How many Ascent Psalms do we find in the Book of Psalms?

Family Discussion Questions:

1. What narrow escapes can we recount in our church? Our country? Our own individual lives?

PSALM 125

Category: *Ascent, Faith*
Occasion: *Rise in Tyranny*
Author: *Unknown*

....

¹ They that trust in the Lord shall be as mount Zion, which cannot be removed, but abideth forever.

² As the mountains are round about Jerusalem, so the Lord is round about His people from henceforth even forever.

³ For the rod of the wicked shall not rest upon the lot of the righteous; lest the righteous put forth their hands unto iniquity.

⁴ Do good, O Lord, unto those that be good, and to them that are upright in their hearts.

⁵ As for such as turn aside unto their crooked ways, the Lord shall lead them forth with the workers of iniquity: but peace shall be upon Israel.

The Point:

God protects the righteous from the corrupting influences and the tyrannical forces of the world.

How do we feel in the recitation of this Psalm?

For a time, it may appear that the church is threatened by extinction because of prolonged persecutions from both apostates and tyrants. When the tyrants have completely enslaved God's people and forced their children into indoctrination programs and exposed them to foul cultural systems, we wonder if the righteous will survive at all. Only if they trust in the Lord.

What does this Psalm say?

Verses 1-2

References to Jerusalem in the Old Testament denote a physical place where God met with His people Israel. That would change with the coming of Christ, as He notes in John 4:23: "The hour cometh when ye shall neither in this mountain nor yet at Jerusalem worship the Father... The hour cometh and now is, when the true worshipers shall worship the Father in spirit and in truth." As the Old Testament saints ascended to Jerusalem for worship, they were reminded of the true Mount Zion. Those that trust in the Lord are "as mount Zion."

As verse one says, there must be something of Mount Zion that cannot be removed. Something abides forever. It is common knowledge that Jerusalem was destroyed twice, and it did not remain forever. If that is the case, then what is it that remains forever, but those people who trust in the Lord?

Verse two contains a comforting promise that the Lord surrounds His people like the mountains surround Jerusalem. Again, this is strong confirmation that the people of God really constitute the figure of Jerusalem. Hebrews 13:5 confirms the promise again for the New Testament saints, "I will never leave thee, nor forsake thee."

Verse 3

Occasionally in history, evil rulers virtually wiped out Christian influence from a land. This is the case with Afghanistan, Iraq, and North Korea in our day, as well as Japan in the 17th century. Forced intermarriage with Muslims wiped out Christian civilization in Turkey and the Middle East during the early middle ages. Thankfully, God provides a way of escape for Christians all over the world. America has served as a refuge for several hundred years, although that appears to be coming to an end now. The Department of State has been very hesitant to allow Christian refugees into the country. Suffice it to say, that God can provide a way of escape for Christians so as to protect a heritage for the future. These tyrannies are short lived, if the kingdom of Christ will continue to prosper through history.

Several years ago, a Christian shopkeeper in Mexico received an unwelcome visit from members of a drug cartel. They threatened his family, revealed that they knew his children's names and other personal information about them. Later that evening he heard a message preached on the deliverance of the children of Israel from Egypt. The verse that remained with him was Exodus 14:13. Speaking of Pharaoh and the Egyptians, Moses said, "Ye shall see them again no more forever!" The next day, as the shopkeeper picked up a newspaper in a coffee shop, he was astonished to see the pictures of the men who had accosted him the day before. Evidently, the police had apprehended them, and to this day the Christian man has seen no sign of the thugs.

The powerful influence of ungodly institutions and demonic forces on the hearts and minds of Christians is also a consideration in this Psalm. When these forces get a foothold in the lives of Christian leaders, these leaders can produce significant damage. Between 2008 and 2014, a number of large evangelical ministries in America were severely compromised when the leaders succumbed to sexual sins. The Roman Catholic Church has been decimated by an unprecedented number of lawsuits and court trials relating to treacherous sexual behavior. These are desperately evil times, when the church is besmirched with the worst filth of the world. Much of this may be traced to the 1960s sexual revolution that unleashed upon the world a destructive, demonic force, destroying the institution of marriage. The rod of the wicked came to rest upon the organized church in many instances.

Verses 4-5

These verses mark out three categories of persons: faithful believers, apostates, and the heathen (called "the workers of iniquity"). The Psalmist requests God's blessings and peace on those who are faithful to the covenant—they are upright in heart and steadfast in faith (by God's grace). As for those who apostatize from the faith, they will degrade into the ways of the heathen. Certainly, we have seen this in our apostate Christian nations where young people everywhere are leaving the church, and increasingly gravitating towards the heathen practices of body mutilation, cannibalism, vampirism, homosexuality, and transvestism. Apostates look more and more like pagans. So in the end, there will always be two groups of people—referred to in Scripture as the wheat and the tares, the sheep and the goats, and the righteous and wicked.

We have the assurance that even in these dreadful times of mass apostasy, there is peace with Israel. God's church does survive, protected from the chaos and destructive forces about it. Peace shall be upon Israel.

How do we apply this Psalm to our lives?

We should take great encouragement that God is sovereign over the great tyrants and the apostasies. These persecutions will not destroy the church entirely, because they are intended to strengthen the church. What does not destroy us will only strengthen us, because the wrath of man will praise God, and whatever excess wrath they wish to express—He will restrain (Ps. 76:10).

How does this Psalm teach us to worship God?

God blesses those who commit to His worship, and He forces those given to worldly influences to repent or leave the church . The preaching of the church should clear the fence-sitters off the fence. Either God's people must commit to His worship and to His service, or they turn aside to their crooked ways.

Questions:

1. What is it about Jerusalem that abides forever?

2. In what countries (recently) has the very existence of the church of Christ been threatened?

3. What is the "Rod of the Wicked?"

4. What happens to apostates who turn aside to crooked ways? How do apostates in the Western world increasingly look like the "workers of iniquity?"

5. In what sense are there only two categories of persons, and in what sense are there three categories of persons (in relation to Christ and the church)?

6. Categorize the Ascent Psalms from Psalm 120 through Psalm 125. Which are Faith Psalms, Deliverance Psalms, and Thanksgiving Psalms?

Family Discussion Questions:

1. Can you think of instances in which God protected His people from the rod of the wicked, in recent experience?

Psalm 126

Category: *Ascent, Thanksgiving*
Occasion: *Church Restoration*
Author: *Unknown*

....

¹ When the Lord turned again the captivity of Zion, we were like them that dream.

² Then was our mouth filled with laughter, and our tongue with singing: then said they among the heathen, The Lord hath done great things for them.

³ The Lord hath done great things for us; whereof we are glad.

⁴ Turn again our captivity, O Lord, as the streams in the south.

⁵ They that sow in tears shall reap in joy.

⁶ He that goeth forth and weepeth, bearing precious seed, shall doubtless come again with rejoicing, bringing his sheaves with him.

The Point:

We count on God's restoration of His church during times of great distress.

How do we feel in the recitation of this Psalm?

After experiencing a low point in the history of the church (and all the grief associated with it), our spirits are wonderfully restored when God chooses to restore and reform the church of Christ. This is a joyful song, where we delight in the blessings of God upon His people.

What does this Psalm say?

Verse 1

The context of this psalm is the Babylonian captivity: the people of God were taken into captivity in Babylon for a period of 70 years. The last remnant of the church was now in exile, and it was a discouraging time (as depicted in Psalm 137). But men and women of faith were still hoping in God, confident that He would restore His people. God's people must have been very encouraged and comforted as they returned from Babylon. After all of their rebellion, and the various tribulations God had brought upon His people over the previous 600 years, now it was apparent that the Lord was willing to "give it another try." This illustrates the covenantal faithfulness of God. For every true believer in Yahweh God, this represented a new start and a reformation of the church.

Have you ever had such a wonderful experience that for a moment you wondered if it could be real? You had to pinch yourself to make sure you weren't dreaming. When God's people sense that reformation is actually happening in their church community, they experience a great sense of joy. It may feel surreal at first. Do you remember the little girl Rhoda in the Book of Acts? When she saw Peter released from prison, she thought she had seen a ghost. At first glance, she could hardly believe that God was answering prayers. These are times of great celebration, when God has restored a remnant of the church and a remnant of authentic faith.

Verses 2–3

The joyful church is a singing church. A singing church provides the greatest testimony to the world around it. When we truly reflect joy by exuberant and loud singing, the world cannot help but notice. In New Testament language, when unbelievers hear the convicting Word of Truth preached and sung, they fall on their faces and worship God, confessing that God is in the midst of these people (1 Cor. 14:25). Unbelievers who are warming to the gospel detect the conviction of the truth, because it is present, because it is manifest in the words and the attitudes and demeanor of the Christians there. Given their joy and their confidence in the resurrection of Christ, God must have done great things for them!

The source of our joy is God's work. We cannot deny that God has done great things for us. What greater things can we think of than transformed lives and new life in Christ?

Verses 4-6

When a plant withers, it retains seeds that will germinate later. And during times of decline in the church, it appears to be dying. These are sad and difficult days, and hopes grow dim. But God in His providential care of the church will not let it disappear off the face of the earth. Every dying plant retains the seeds, and the "dead" seeds were carried into the Babylonian captivity. God wasn't finished with His people at this point, for they would come back to the land with Ezra and Nehemiah. However depressing these times may be for the church, the seeds themselves bear hope. We hope for future rejoicing, knowing that the seeds will one day bear fruit again.

How do we apply this Psalm to our lives?

If the church is declining and dying in the Western world (England, Scotland, Canada, and America) or anywhere else, we must continue to hope that God will one day germinate the seeds again. Some day, the endless denominational fracturing will end. Some day, the pattern of moral apostasy and spiritual apostasy will reverse its direction. Some day, shallow and man-centered worship will be replaced with God-centered, worship-in-Spirit-and-truth again. The seeds themselves retain hope even in these times of grief.

Perhaps the seeds will go with missionaries and exiles from the Western countries into other nations that have less access to the Gospel of Christ. They may produce more fruit in these foreign nations than in the apostate, hard-hearted Western world

How does this Psalm teach us to worship God?

Occasionally, the local church emerges out of periods of decline and apostasy into Spirit-filled revival. These are times of rejoicing, for we know that any evidence of spiritual life is nothing less than a supernatural work of the Spirit.

Questions:

1. What is the context of this psalm?

2. Who brought the sheaves back to Jerusalem after the exile?

3. What makes this such a joyful time?

4. What two groups recognize the goodness of God upon the people of God (according to verses 2 and 3)?

5. How can we be sure that Christ's church will never completely die out?

Family Discussion Questions:

1. In what places is the church in decline today, and where is the church experiencing tremendous growth?

Psalm 127

Category: *Ascent, Faith*
Occasion: *Building a Home*
Author: *Solomon*

....

1 Except the Lord build the house, they labour in vain that build it: except the Lord keep the city, the watchman waketh but in vain.

2 It is vain for you to rise up early, to sit up late, to eat the bread of sorrows: for so He giveth His beloved sleep.

3 Lo, children are an heritage of the Lord: and the fruit of the womb is His reward.

4 As arrows are in the hand of a mighty man; so are children of the youth.

5 Happy is the man that hath his quiver full of them: they shall not be ashamed, but they shall speak with the enemies in the gate.

The Point:

Those building cities and homes must trust in the Lord, believe that their children are a blessing, and that they will be a blessing in their generation.

How do we feel in the recitation of this Psalm?

Peace and happiness. There is so much we cannot control about our family, our children, and our nation. We certainly cannot sovereignly ordain the outcome of any and all events. When we remember that

God is in control, we can sleep peacefully. And when we look at our children, we are reminded that God has given us these gifts. We are recipients of the kindnesses of God and we are happy.

What does this Psalm say?

Verses 1-2

How will a city survive, if there are no watchmen and no men to defend it? How will a house be built, if men do not build it? How will our children be raised, if we do not raise them? This psalm introduces the apparent paradox of God's sovereignty and human responsibility. Who builds the house and who defends the city from marauders? Most people will say that a father and a mother build the house, and soldiers defend the city or country. However, this psalm calls for God to build the house and watch over the city. All is vain if the Lord's hand is not in it. Of course, the Lord does not build the house with hammers or keep the city with guns and surface-to-air missiles. His hand is active in a thousand different ways. But if He chooses not to protect the city or bless our covenant households, then all of our work is vain. All the military armaments in the world cannot protect a city or a nation that God assigns to destruction.

Given that God builds the house, we had better look to God for His work in our homes and churches. Though our hands may be busy doing the work of building homes and church communities, our eyes must be fastened upon the hands of God to do the real work. It is only God that can guarantee any success of our work.

One of the best tests of faith is found in sleeping. Troubles with sleeping oftentimes are connected to weakness in faith. When a person comes to think, "everything depends on me," he will soon find that he cannot rest well. Who will watch over all of his responsibilities while he sleeps? This is an important test as to whether or not we really do believe that God retains absolute control over all things.

Verse 3

At a time when 99% of women use birth control and the worldwide birth rate has plummeted from 5.0% to 2.5% since 1960, it is harder to find families who agree with this statement: "Children are a blessing from God." This passage does not command couples to produce a certain number of children per family. However, there is this statement of indicative truth: Children are an heritage of the Lord, and the fruit of the womb is His reward. Christian churches that see the average birth rate within their communities falling from 3.0 to 1.5 ought to be concerned that God may be withholding His blessings. This, however, is not the way many see it. According to the Guttmacher Institute, 73% of evangelical Christians and 68% of Roman Catholics use a high-efficiency form of birth control. Are Christians giving way to the materialism and self-centeredness of the day? While there is no mandate for a family to have "as many children as possible," or "adopt as many children as possible," Christian parents ought to receive children into their families as God's good gifts. If a nation's birth rate drops to half of what it was over the last one hundred years, while the square footage of the average house has doubled in size, we must conclude that this nation prefers drywall to babies. A preference for material wealth and a convenient lifestyle has trumped the kingdom of God and His righteousness in the minds of many Western Christians.

Verses 4-5

These verses reveal more of the blessings that come with children. A skilled and powerful warrior does well when he is armed with plenty of ammunition, arrows, and grenades. These armaments facilitate what he does best. This is the picture used for the children that sit around the kitchen table in a God-fearing home. Children raised in the covenant home become useful in the hands of Christ. Remember, Christ is robbing the rich man's house and building His own kingdom. Verse five speaks of strength, courage, and unity. When brothers are bound together by blood and by Christ, there is a special strength and courage that forms against the enemy: the world, the flesh, and the devil. In some cases, our children will take leadership in the gates as pastors or civil leaders. The gates represent the place of leadership (whether in church or state). In this capacity, they exhibit even more courage when they take on the antithesis.

Note also that these are arrows in the hand of Christ, the ultimate "mighty man." These arrows cannot achieve anything apart from the mighty One who deploys them to the benefit of His Kingdom. May God give us children who are dangerous to the enemy, and useful to the King of kings who must reign until all of His enemies are under His footstool!

How do we apply this Psalm to our lives?

Let us be very careful not to think of ourselves as sovereignly determining the state of our family. We can fail at a thousand points. Any lapse, spiritual or practical, could produce dire consequences. You can be the very best automobile driver and still be involved in a fatal accident just one hour from now. So let us trust in God. Let us believe that He will work all things for good, because He truly has "the whole wide world in His hands."

The greatest enemy exhibits itself in the form of ideas (2 Cor. 10:4, 5). Where young men and women are trained carefully in biblical thinking, they are equipped to oppose the ideas of humanists, evolutionists, feminists, existentialists, Unitarians, and others that have undermined the faith in the Western world. These battles are fought in the universities, the churches, the media, and in the publishing industry. May God raise up powerful weapons in our own homes against these forces.

How does this Psalm teach us to worship God?

The Lord builds His church. In the ultimate sense, we have no control over who will attend our church, who will be faithful, and who will be unfaithful. We have no control over who will listen to the sermon and apply it, and who will not. We have no control over which children will apostatize and which will not. "On this rock," says Jesus, "I will build My church." Peter doesn't build the church, and neither do we. Our great wisdom and powerful personalities are of little use when we are set against the sinful hearts of men. When we gather together, let us remember that it is the Lord that has assembled these living stones. Not us.

Questions:

1. How does this Psalm speak of the Sovereignty of God? Do armies guard our country, or does God guard our country?

2. What is one of the best tests of true faith?

3. What has happened to the worldwide birth rate since 1960?

4. How are we to think about our children?

5. What does it mean to "speak with the enemy in the gates?"

Family Discussion Questions:

1. Does our family rest in God's sovereignty, or are we more inclined to rely on our own efforts as we build our home?

2. Why are people less inclined to have children in our day? Which of these are good and godly motives, and which are ungodly motives?

Psalm 128

Category: *Faith, Ascent*
Occasion: *The Blessed Life*
Author: *Unknown*

....

1 Blessed is every one that feareth the Lord; that walketh in His ways.
2 For thou shalt eat the labour of thine hands: happy shalt thou be, and it shall be well with thee.
3 Thy wife shall be as a fruitful vine by the sides of thine house: thy children like olive plants round about thy table.
4 Behold, that thus shall the man be blessed that feareth the Lord.
5 The Lord shall bless thee out of Zion: and thou shalt see the good of Jerusalem all the days of thy life.
6 Yea, thou shalt see thy children's children, and peace upon Israel.

The Point:

The beginning of wisdom is the fear of the Lord, and all of the blessings that come to a family and church are based on fearing the Lord.

How do we feel in the recitation of this Psalm?

We fear God and we are happy. We don't fear God and we are unhappy: we are pulled apart by all of our anxieties and a thousand competing "fears." When we fear God, we do not fear circumstances, apostasy, character assassination, teenage rebellion, economic ruin, divorce, or even death. We are too busy fearing God to fear any of these things.

What does this Psalm say?

Verse 1

Clearly, this psalm is directed to a father and a husband. This is not uncharacteristic of the Scriptures, as the Ten Commandments read, "Thou shalt not covet thy neighbor's wife," but says nothing about coveting "thy neighbor's husband." God puts concerted weight upon the father of the home. Where fatherhood breaks down in a certain community, and where the fathers do not fear God, bad things can happen.

All of the subsequent blessings mentioned in the psalm hinge upon this first verse (repeated in verse four): "Blessed is the man that fears the Lord and walks in His ways." The father that attends worship services on a Sunday but habitually visits illicit websites is not fearing God. Though he may carry on his sinful habits in secret, the true character of his life will be evident to all. It is not uncommon that the sins a father commits in secret are committed openly by his sons. However, the man who has learned to fear God and to walk in His ways can expect the blessings enumerated in this psalm. Thus, we conclude that the fear of God is the very root of the good life, and the beginning of wisdom. How can a man know if he fears God? His actions will be motivated by this central concern. He cannot bear the violation of God's name in his presence. He quickly confesses his sins and repents when he discovers that he has displeased God. This becomes the pattern of the man's life, as he is renewed by the grace of God. Without God's grace, we would still be blinded in sin and incapable of perceiving God in a right manner.

Verses 2-4

Men who fear God are happy men. To the carnal mind, the fear of God is dull, even abhorrent. They wonder how fearing God could produce any happiness whatsoever. So they seek happiness through the party life, drunkenness, and stuffing their faces with excessive "pleasures." They pursue self-worship and other forms of idolatry. Then they live with the fear of man, the torture of guilt, the pain of hangovers, and the heavy pall of death. This is not the life of happiness. If they had feared God, they would have found happiness. Instead, they find nothing but grief, bitterness, and corruption.

It is one thing to earn a living and obtain significant wealth. But it is quite another thing to enjoy the fruits of one's labors, with maximum happiness and fulfillment of joy. Only God can provide us this added benefit. Most rich people are miserable because their hearts are set on the uncertain riches—they worship the wrong god.

The greatest earthly blessing is not the produce of our hands or the achievement of status and fame. It is the blessing of a good wife and fruitful children, who are described as olive plants in verse three. As olive plants do not yield their fruit for five to eight years after planting, we may not see fruit right away from our efforts in child training. We should be ready to provide many years of spiritual, academic, and practical, economic training before our children will yield fruit like a mature olive tree.

This psalm also assumes the existence of the family economy. At one time in human history, children were not considered a product of the state. They were not considered a financial drag on the household, as they are today. Media pundits and sociologists warn families that each additional child will cost them over $300,000. However, the writer of this psalm sees something of a potential for wealth in a God-fearing family blessed with children.

Of course, as Christians we are more interested in the kingdom of God than we are in material benefits and comforts for ourselves. We do not mind a little sacrifice of our own wealth and comfort for our children. But more than this, we are interested in discipling our little "nations" (Matt. 28:18), as God provides us this opportunity to serve His kingdom. We see our children as mighty servants in the hands of Christ the King. This is ultimate productivity!

John Adams succeeded in becoming president of the United States, but two of his sons became a terrible grief to him in his later years. Paris Hilton was an heir of the great Hilton Hotel wealth, but by her profligate lifestyle, she besmirched her grandfather's legacy. From these and other examples, we can see that wealth and power pale in significance when compared to the spiritual and economic legacy carried on in the lives of children and grandchildren.

Verses 5-6

God's people considered the church to be the greatest joy on earth. Nothing thrills the soul of God's man more than to see the progress, the advancement, and the strengthening of the church. He does not want to see the church languishing. In fact, the end game for all of life on earth must be the prosperity of Mount Zion—the church of the firstborn, the city of the living God (Heb. 12:22, 23). Men who fear God will see this blessing in their communities. And of course, as already included in the other ascent psalms, we find this psalm extolling the blessing of peace and unity within the body of the church (verse six).

How do we apply this Psalm to our lives?

- What about the husband who does not see his wife as a fruitful vine? Perhaps he flirts with the idea that he "married the wrong woman." The fact is that every man gets the wife that God gives to him, and every woman gets the husband that God gives to her. The problems in our marriages are always rooted in our perspective of God and our relationship to God. By nature, men and women do not fear God, and they do not delight greatly in the commandments of God. If we want our households to become something like what we find in verse three of this psalm, we must study what it means to fear God and walk in His ways.

- Covenant blessings for the godly family will only flow from the church of Jesus Christ. Occasionally, families will attempt to separate themselves from the church. It seems that no church is good enough for them, so they give up on it. If they give up on the church, they walk away from the fount from which blessings flow (verse five). While the apostate churches have increased in number, this should in no way discourage us from our search for the biblically-based, historically-rooted Christian church.

How does this Psalm teach us to worship God?

The basic building block of the God-worshiping church body is the man who fears God and expresses it in family worship. It is one thing to talk of the fear of God on Sunday morning, but that talk does not mean anything if a man is not living in the fear of God the rest of the week. As fathers and husbands, let us study the fear of God, talk as if we fear God, sing the fear of God, and live out the fear of God every day.

Questions:

1. What is the great condition upon which the blessings presented in this psalm must stand?

2. To whom is this psalm directed? To whom is the tenth commandment directed?

3. What are the blessings promised in the psalm?

4. To what are our children compared in verse three? Why does this apply to children in the covenant family?

5. What is our highest desire and joy on earth?

Family Discussion Questions:

1. How do we express the fear of God in our home? How does Dad exemplify fear of God throughout the week?

2. How has God blessed our home? What are the highest blessings among all these blessings with which we are blessed?

PSALM 129

Category: *Imprecatory, Ascent*
Occasion: *Enemies Hating the Church*
Author: *Unknown*

....

1   Many a time have they afflicted me from my youth, may Israel
    now say:
2   Many a time have they afflicted me from my youth: yet they have
    not prevailed against me.
3   The plowers plowed upon my back: they made long their furrows.
4   The Lord is righteous: He hath cut asunder the cords of the
    wicked.
5   Let them all be confounded and turned back that hate Zion.
6   Let them be as the grass upon the housetops, which withereth
    afore it groweth up:
7   Wherewith the mower filleth not his hand; nor he that bindeth
    sheaves his bosom.
8   Neither do they which go by say, The blessing of the Lord be
    upon you: we bless you in the name of the Lord.

The Point:

Those that hate God's people also hate God, but they have picked
the wrong fight!

How do we feel in the recitation of this Psalm?

We are distressed to see the relentless persecution of the precious people of God through the centuries. These opponents of the true church appear formidable, their influence unstoppable. For the honor and the glory of God, however, we will not give these opponents the favor of even the slightest bit of awe or dread. Rather, we will loudly declare their eventual defeat. We are utterly convinced that all that oppose Christ will sink into the deepest mire of ignominy and shame forever.

What does this Psalm say?

Verses 1-3

On his way up to assemble with the saints, the psalmist here reflects on the history of the church (God's people). Perhaps he is imminently aware of the more recent news reports of Christians slain for their faith in North Korea, Pakistan, or Eritrea. If he has read the newspapers lately, he has sensed the enemy's utter spite for those who stand for Christ and His righteous law.

The text of this psalm is put in the first person ("I," "Me," "My") because we identify with this church and its persecutions as if they are doing it to us. "The wicked have plowed deep furrows up and down my back." They have whipped the back of the church of Christ a thousand times over thousands of years. The scars are visible everywhere. Sometimes the wounds appear in real physical form on the backs of our brothers and sisters around the world.

This sight especially disturbs us when we consider the object of their persecutions. These abusers want to get at the Lord Jesus Christ, so they take it out on His bride. They would take a baseball bat to the face of Christ's bride. Suppose a ruffian entered a wedding service and commenced to beating on the bride as she entered the building. How do you think the bridegroom would respond to this? How would the rest of the guests view such degrading treatment of the bride? This is the sentiment felt in these verses.

Verse 4

At this point in the psalm, the psalmist begins to see things from

God's perspective. How does God view the rough treatment of His children? If we are concerned by justice, God is the very standard of justice. There is nobody in the universe or outside of it more committed to righteousness than this thrice-holy God. We must be careful not to think of God as disinterested in His people. He has already shown His power, justice, and mercy in history. Look at what He did to Pharaoh in Egypt! Look at what He did to the persecuting forces of Rome! Look at what He did to Ceausescu of Romania, more recently! There will be an end for every persecutor of the true church of Christ. God's people are released from the bonds of Satan, their own sin, and the bonds of the world again and again throughout history.

Verses 5–8

These last verses contain the imprecatory element of the psalm. These are prayers that God will bring the purposes and actions of the wicked to nothing. Of course, He will do this. He cannot help but do this. Does anybody really believe that the liberal seminaries, powerful persecuting governments, or divisive wolves in local churches can one-up Jesus Christ as He builds His church? At first glance, these forces appear formidable. After all, they dominate most of the institutions in the Western world. They have established themselves over 200-400 years. But the psalmist knows they are short-lived and futile efforts. They are nothing but weeds growing in the thin layer of dirt found on rooftops (verse six). In the olden days, roofs of houses were often made of mud and thatch. A few weeds might sprout up here and there on these rooftops, but there was never a substantive root system. Nobody was going to harvest a crop on these roofs! (verse seven). North Korean and Chinese governments have persecuted the church in the Far East relentlessly for fifty years, but they will soon be dead and gone, and the church will be stronger than ever. Every deterrent to the church will only strengthen it over time.

How do we apply this Psalm to our lives?

How does this psalm comport with Jesus' admonition to "bless those that curse you?" 2 John 10 warns us not to receive a deceiver into the house or to bid him "Godspeed." Paul also warns of Alexander the coppersmith who withstood the teaching of the Apostles (in 2 Tim. 4:14,15). He even goes so far as to issue a curse on anybody who should pervert the gospel and corrupt the churches of Galatia (Gal. 1:6-9). This doesn't sound much like "blessing those that curse you." However, here the concern is not what these persecutors will do to me "personally." It is the damage they will do to the church body. Paul is jealous over the church of Corinth, the betrothed of Christ in 2 Corinthians 11:1-4, such that he warns them against those who preach the wrong Christ. Thus, it is right and appropriate that we pray a curse upon the Mormon church, the liberal Protestant seminary, and any and all powerful institutions that work hard to destroy Christ's church and its influence.

How does this Psalm teach us to worship God?

Let us cultivate a holy jealousy in our hearts towards the church of Christ. Wherever there is a lackadaisical approach to the church, or a general disinterest in the struggle for truth and unity in the church, you will find apostasy. This holy jealousy must be seen in passionate prayers to God, like what we find in this psalm. There may be a tinge of bitterness, even, and holy hatred towards the forces that afflict the church. That's appropriate as long as it does not cross over into self-preservation and self-aggrandizement.

Questions:

1. Whose back has been scarred by the afflictions of the wicked?

2. What is an imprecatory prayer? Can you name several other imprecatory psalms?

3. What happens to grass that sprouts on the rooftops of houses, or in the cracks of sidewalks?

4. What did God do to Pharaoh in Egypt, and Ceausescu of Romania?

5. Against whom does the Apostle Paul levy a curse in Galatians 1?

Family Discussion Questions:

1. How do we feel when we read about the forces that are trying to destroy the true church in America or North Korea?

2. Against whom might we pray an imprecatory prayer? Describe the right way and a wrong way to pray a prayer like this.

Psalm 130

Category: *Faith, Ascent*
Occasion: *Long Term Isolation/Imprisonment*
Author: *Unknown*

....

1 Out of the depths have I cried unto thee, O Lord.
2 Lord, hear my voice: let thine ears be attentive to the voice of my
   supplications.
3 If thou, Lord, shouldest mark iniquities, O Lord, who shall
   stand?
4 But there is forgiveness with thee, that thou mayest be feared.
5 I wait for the Lord, my soul doth wait, and in His word do I
   hope.
6 My soul waiteth for the Lord more than they that watch for the
   morning: I say, more than they that watch for the morning.
7 Let Israel hope in the Lord: for with the Lord there is mercy, and
   with Him is plenteous redemption.
8 And He shall redeem Israel from all his iniquities.

The Point:

Though we may be cast away in isolation or imprisonment for an
extended period of time, we still hold tenaciously to the promises we
have received from the Word of God.

How do we feel in the recitation of this Psalm?

We feel as though we are in a very dark and very deep dungeon, far away from any immediate aid. Nonetheless, we are confident that God hears our prayers. All the verses, all the promises we have learned from God's Word, come rushing into our minds, and we are strengthened by them

What does this Psalm say?

Verses 1–2

The writer of this psalm may be in a dungeon, or perhaps he is in the belly of a large fish at the bottom of the sea. He may be sitting under multiple layers of emotional torment, demonic assaults, or depressing thoughts. He may be approaching physical death, or feeling that he is sinking about as low as the grave. For the Christian, the grave is the lowest he will ever go. As we shall discover, the psalmist's concerns are more spiritual than physical.

The desperate cry to God that we find in this psalm is the only cry that makes sense when faced with the prospect of death. To whom can we appeal other than the Giver of Life? A friend may help you pull a sliver from your foot. He may give you a lift to the grocery store. But who will deliver you from death and the grave? When we realize the threat of spiritual and physical death, we can only cry out to God. Our appeals are in dead earnest. There is no half-hearted rote in this. Our appeals are direct, sincere, and faith-filled. We are speaking to God, and we beg His ear: "Lord, hear my voice!"

Verses 3–4

From the outset of this prayer, we find strong faith and a robust encouragement. Right away, the psalmist goes to the greatest news of all—the promise of the forgiveness of God. If God were to hold our sins against us, we would be done for. What a terrible predicament for us! Not one person could defend himself in the courtroom of God. No lawyer could ever make the case. There would be no acquittals. Natural man wants to believe that sin is not a big deal, that God is willing to ignore a little sinful indiscretion here and there. But of course, this is nothing but wishful thinking.

The good news comes in verse four, with that magnificent little conjunction: "But" (see also Eph. 2:4). Thankfully, we are not left to the retributions of God's wrath and justice. This is a huge relief! He forgives us of our sins. He does not hold our sins against us because of the sacrificial work of His Son, the Lord Jesus Christ, on the cross (2 Cor. 5:19). The Son of God was made to be sin for us, that we might be made the righteousness of God in Him (2 Cor. 5:21). Although the Old Testament saints did not understand the basis for God's mercy before Jesus came, they accepted the promise of forgiveness. They knew and believed that God would forgive their sins.

What is to be made of the highly unusual statement at the end of verse four? What does forgiveness have to do with the fear of God? Here is the connection. Those who have by faith realized God's forgiveness are the least likely to deny their offense. How can you be forgiven if you have never offended? The magnitude of the pardon signifies the magnitude of the offense. If you offend a dog, it is hardly a concern. It is far more egregious to offend the president of the country, but even more so the Creator of the Universe. So once we have realized the magnitude of our offense, and the blessing of that sin forgiven, we cannot help but fear God and rejoice with trembling (Ps. 2:11). If you have ever survived a near-miss traffic accident you know something of this sentiment. Perhaps your car stalled on the train tracks, and you were able to push the vehicle off the tracks seconds before the train made the intersection. Or maybe you rolled to safety away from a speeding semi truck. For a few moments, your whole body trembles for having barely escaped a dreadful predicament. Great relief sweeps over your being. This is a faint comparison to our near avoidance of God's eternal judgment.

Verses 5-8

While it is a great relief to receive the forgiveness of sins, the believer is still crying out from the depths. His present condition does not feel very much like heaven. Think about the Christian sitting in a filthy prison cell in North Korea. Under these circumstances, all he has in his mind is a few Bible verses, a few promises from God. He has the promise of sins forgiven and the promise of resurrection. These may not seem like present realities, as he suffers under the evil consequences of a sinful world (pain, torture, and death). Now, he can do two things—he can wait on the Lord and he can hope in His Word. Over and over again, he reminds himself of the promises of God. He speaks the promises of God to others. He prays the promises of God. He hangs all of his hopes upon these promises, and this gives him comfort. Then, he believes that there is plenteous redemption with God. He tells the other prisoners, "God is going to get us out of here." As the years go by, some of the prisoners doubt more and more, but not the believer. He refuses to give up on the hope that God will redeem him, and God will save His people from sin and all the effects of it, including death.

How do we apply this Psalm to our lives?

Most problems cannot be solved immediately. By God's wise providence, we still must deal with the problems of disease and death. We still struggle through the various trials, doubts, depressions, and persecutions day by day. Yet in this state, we can hope in God's salvation—that He will eventually pull us out of it. We can learn joy in sorrow, because there is a rock-bottom hope that takes us through it. This marks the heart attitude of the Christian.

How does this Psalm teach us to worship God?

Christian worship is hopeful worship. We speak aloud the promises of God. We encourage each other to believe them. Like Christians assembling in a prison camp every day, we are corporately waiting for God's salvation. Together we hope in God. Together we wait for Him to send His special forces to rescue us from our predicament. It is the most hopeful saints that will be leading worship in the prison camp!

Questions:

1. Where is the psalmist as he prays this prayer? What is his situation?

2. What is the greatest news of all, shared in this psalm?

3. How does God's forgiveness inspire fear?

4. What are the two things we can do while suffering in this present world?

5. According to the last verse, from what will God save all of His people?

Family Discussion Questions:

1. How do we react when things go badly for us?

2. Are we hopeful in the midst of serious trial and temptation? Who are the most hopeful people in our church?

PSALM 131

Category: *Faith, Ascent*
Occasion: *Humbled*
Author: *David*

....

¹ Lord, my heart is not haughty, nor mine eyes lofty: neither do I
   exercise myself in great matters, or in things too high for me.
² Surely I have behaved and quieted myself, as a child that is
   weaned of his mother: my soul is even as a weaned child.
³ Let Israel hope in the Lord from henceforth and forever.

The Point:

We have the faith of little children, even nursing babies that trust
their mothers for their lives.

How do we feel in the recitation of this Psalm?

When a little six-month-old child has finished nursing, he content-
edly rolls over and closes his eyes for a little nap. No worries. No
fears. No sorrows. He has all that he needs at least for the moment,
and he trusts his life in his mother's arms. We are humbled as we
identify with this six-month-old child.

What does this Psalm say?

Verse 1

There is nothing more winsome than a genuine humility. There is nothing more approachable than humility. Scripture tells us that God Himself is attracted to this grace: "God resists the proud, but giveth grace to the humble" (Jas. 4:6). Humility is seeing ourselves as God sees us, as we really stand in relation to God and the rest of reality. As a two-year-old wanders through a crowd of adults, all he can see is a sea of big shoes, socks, and knees. He know these are big people and he is a little person. He does not understand the adult conversation going on. All of this adult life is literally over his head. If we were honest with ourselves, we would admit that there is much going on around us that we do not understand. There are problems in the universe that we cannot possibly solve. There are apparent paradoxes we will never resolve. There are limits to our understanding. For example, a two-year-old may have learned to hit a switch to turn on the lights in the living room. But he doesn't know how electrons flowing through a wire lighten the filament, and he certainly doesn't understand what excites these electrons and enables them to travel through the wires. Scientists are still trying to understand the nature of the electron itself. Albert Einstein was one of the most brilliant men of our times, yet he was known for his childish antics. He had something of a picture of the incomprehensibility of God's universe when he would say, "The human mind, no matter how highly trained, cannot grasp the universe. We are in the position of a little child, entering a huge library whose walls are covered to the ceiling with books in many different tongues."

The more we learn of the universe, the more we should exemplify the heart attitude that David brings to this psalm. Generally, a two-year-old child is content to not know everything there is to know. He takes it as a given that adults are smarter than he is. However, as we grow up, many of us face the temptation to explain mysteries beyond our level of comprehension. This temptation is the basis for all of the false philosophies and cults that man has concocted through the ages. The Russellites of the 19th Century could not explain the unity of God, the deity of the persons, and the distinct personalities of the Father, Son, and Holy Spirit. So they handily "fixed" the whole problem by taking the deity of the persons away. They gave in to the temptation. Human rationalism exercises itself in great matters, things too high for man. The root problem with the cults is pride. May God obliterate every vestige of pride that plagues the church! When it comes to the matter of the doctrine of God, we must be very careful never to go beyond what God has given to us in His Word.

Denominationalism within the church is rooted in the pride of men, especially in this area of knowledge. In doctrinal disagreements with another party, we should first acknowledge what we do not know— the unexplained mysteries and apparent paradoxes of our systems. Then, together with the other party, we must reaffirm what we know for certain and the things we can agree upon. Only after these exercises are complete, should we gingerly work into some of the perceived disagreements. If this process is used, there will be far less fracturing in the unity of the organized church.

Verse 2

Following this confession of childlike humility comes this wonderful picture of a childlike faith. Faith brings a contentedness, a sense that all is right in our world. We are well taken care of. We are in good hands. We have all that we need, because it is the Lord who determines what we need.

Anxieties arise over those things with which we have no ultimate control. Actually, nothing is under our absolute control. We cannot possibly guarantee the outcome of a single endeavor—not one. A nursing child understands this. He doesn't understand much of anything else. But he knows that he is entirely dependent upon his mother for his very sustenance. He cannot wash his clothes. He cannot plant crops. He cannot find the bathroom. Even a Christian corporate president or a great political leader should realize his limitations. If he trusts in God with the outcome of every situation and every decision, he should be free of all anxiety and fear of the future. Although we take responsibility for the work God gives to us, we cannot guarantee the outcome of any one thing we do. We cannot control all of the forces in the universe that act upon us. That is God's job.

Verse 3

This simple little psalm closes with the basis of contentment, the hope of Israel. A little child can see his mother and he can feel his mother. The believer however, hopes in the God who keeps His covenants and holds true to His promises. We read His promises as a child receives his mother's milk. Then, we hold on to that promise as we fall asleep. If we carry these promises in a tight grip, all will be well with our souls as we approach the final judgment day. He has promised that He will save those who believe in Christ, and He cannot possibly break that promise. Every other person in the whole world may let us down, but not so this covenant-keeping God. "Let Israel hope in the LORD from henceforth and forever!"

How do we apply this Psalm to our lives?

When it comes to knowledge, we are called to be good children. When Dad tells us to turn on the lights, we turn on the lights. We don't need to know everything about electricity to act on the knowledge that Dad has given us. This is the essence of the Christian view of knowledge. God teaches us some things about Himself and His creation. We are content with what we receive, and our responsibility is to be obedient children with what we do know.

How does this Psalm teach us to worship God?

Humility is the most basic requirement in the worship of God. If we cannot picture ourselves as 20 two-year-olds sitting in a circle, learning about Jesus for the first time, we have lost perspective. The spirit of pride will utterly ruin the worship service. This is especially true for the pastors and elders who lead. Where there is the spirit of preeminence, an unwillingness to submit to one another, or a hesitation to confess sins one to another, the Spirit of worship is quenched.

Questions:

1. What is humility?

2. Why are children humble (at least in the area of knowledge)?

3. What is a good way to handle doctrinal disagreements?

4. How does a little baby feel after nursing?

5. Why is sleep a good test of faith?

Family Discussion Questions:

1. If we could quantify all of the knowledge in the universe, what percentage of that knowledge do we possess right now? What percentage will we obtain before we die?

2. Are we filled with anxieties and unable to rest, or are we able to sleep without fear or worry?

PSALM 132

Category: *Didactic, Ascent*
Occasion: *Church in Disarray*
Author: *Unknown*

....

1 Lord, remember David, and all his afflictions:
2 How he sware unto the Lord, and vowed unto the mighty God of Jacob;
3 Surely I will not come into the tabernacle of my house, nor go up into my bed;
4 I will not give sleep to mine eyes, or slumber to mine eyelids,
5 Until I find out a place for the Lord, an habitation for the mighty God of Jacob.
6 Lo, we heard of it at Ephratah: we found it in the fields of the wood.
7 We will go into His tabernacles: we will worship at His footstool.
8 Arise, O Lord, into thy rest; thou, and the ark of thy strength.
9 Let thy priests be clothed with righteousness; and let thy saints shout for joy.
10 For thy servant David's sake turn not away the face of thine anointed.
11 The Lord hath sworn in truth unto David; He will not turn from it; of the fruit of thy body will I set upon thy throne.
12 If thy children will keep my covenant and my testimony that I shall teach them, their children shall also sit upon thy throne for evermore.
13 For the Lord hath chosen Zion; He hath desired it for His

habitation.

14 This is my rest for ever: here will I dwell; for I have desired it.

15 I will abundantly bless her provision: I will satisfy her poor with bread.

16 I will also clothe her priests with salvation: and her saints shall shout aloud for joy.

17 There will I make the horn of David to bud: I have ordained a lamp for mine anointed.

18 His enemies will I clothe with shame: but upon himself shall his crown flourish.

The Point:

God has established a place where His people become kings and priests and where He is worshiped.

How do we feel in the recitation of this Psalm?

Our chief interest is to assemble in the tabernacle of God. We carry the spirit of David with us as we come to worship. With all that was in him, David vowed that he would find a place for the worship of God, for meeting with God. As we read this psalm, we redouble our commitments to build the church of Jesus Christ, the Son of David. This becomes our central focus, our life's goal, our chief passion, and our greatest cause for joy. We rejoice as we anticipate meeting with God in the company of the saints.

What does this Psalm say?

Verses 1-5

In order to follow the psalm through, the reader needs to pay attention to who is speaking. The first ten verses consist of our prayer to God. We recall David's commitment to building the temple, but the point is that we identify with David. We resonate with his sentiment, in his passion to build a temple to God. Don't miss David's tremendous dedication to this task. He prioritized God's house over His own. This establishes the priority of the church (or Christ) over our families. To prioritize the church is not to denigrate the family or to negate the responsibilities a man has to his own home. For example, an elder must rule his family well first, before he can rule in the household of God (1 Tim. 3:5). Nonetheless, the goal of building a faithful family is in order to build the body of the church. We do not build a family for the sake of the family. We build a family for the sake of the church. Jesus said, "If any man come to me, and hate not his father, and mother, and wife, and children, and brethren, and sisters, yea, and his own life also, he cannot be my disciple" (Luke 14:26). This establishes the priority of Christ's body (the body of believers) over the family. Our task is to raise our children in the "nurture and admonition of the Lord," with the intent that they will be part of that body of Christ.

"I will not give sleep to mine eyes, or slumber to mine eyelids, until I find out a place for the Lord. . ." There is a certain spirit of desperation and insistence about these verses. There comes a point in a man's life in which he will do or die. He commits himself to the task. He knows that he must do it. That is the spirit David brings to the project of building the temple. He refuses to sleep until he has found a place for the house of God. Truly, God meets with His people in the assembly of the saints, and this then becomes the chief interest of every godly family.

Verses 6-7

The place in which the psalm is written, from which David cries, is Bethlehem (Ephratah) and Kirjathjearim ("the fields of the wood"). In 1 Chronicles 13:1-14, we find the ark of God sitting in the house of Uzzah in Kirjathjearim, about fifteen miles outside of Jerusalem. The worship of God was in disrepair, and had been so since the Philistines had captured the ark some forty years earlier. For some reason, the people of God did not consider the worship of Yahweh a priority (even though the ark of the covenant signified the place at which God met with his people in the Old Testament). So the church languished. At times, the church of the Lord Jesus Christ also suffers neglect. It may be that the elders have other priorities, such as making money and providing for their own comforts. They may do very little discipling, and accountability and discipline fall apart. The teaching becomes rote and unchallenging, conflicts constantly split their church bodies, programs replace relationship, and corporate structures and slick presentations keep the masses happy.

While all this is going on, it is the bride of Christ that suffers. Now, when David walks up and down in Bethlehem and finds the present situation untenable, unacceptable, and even despicable, he must act. It is time to re-prioritize the church in the estimation of God's people. We cannot put it off any longer.

Verses 8-10

Now we pray for a return of the presence of God by His Spirit into the worship. We pray that He will come into the rest that He instituted from the beginning. Our Sabbath rest is in Christ, and it is principally experienced on the first day of the week when we gather as God's people. Where two or three are gathered in His name, Christ promised that He would be in the midst. Therefore, when we gather it is appropriate to invoke the name of Christ. We invite Him into our presence, to the end that we would be clothed in righteousness and respond in joyful worship. These are the two signs that the Spirit of Christ is within us. We enjoy the imputed righteousness (justification), and the infused righteousness (sanctification) of God in Jesus Christ. Then, we let loose a rousing shout of faith-filled joy that God has shown Himself to us, that Christ has redeemed us from our enemies, that we are delivered from the pains of hell to the glories of heaven forever. Verse ten speaks of David and "His Anointed," which must be David's Son, our Lord Jesus Christ.

Verses 11-13

These verses teach us of the covenant that God made with David concerning his monarchical line. It is usually referred to as the "Davidic covenant." Generally, monarchies remain within the family from generation to generation. For various reasons, however, it is rare to see the throne continue within a single line for more than five to ten generations. For example, the Stuart dynasty in England failed after eighty years, ending with the Glorious Revolution of William and Mary. The longest monarchical succession among earthly kingdoms is the Japanese Jimmu dynasty that dates back to 660 BC. David's kingdom exceeds that of the Japanese emperor. The house of Saul failed after a single generation, and Jeroboam's monarchy in the northern kingdom ended with Jehu. But God promised that David's monarchy would continue in his house forever. Verse twelve notes that this promise is dependent upon the "keeping of the covenant."

Only one descendant of David was able to keep the testimonies of God perfectly, and that was the Lord Jesus Christ. Thus, our Lord becomes the fulfillment of the Davidic covenant. He was installed on the throne of David in AD 33, and he must reign until all of his enemies are put under his footstool (1 Cor. 15:25).

Verses 14-18

The psalm turns a corner in verse 14, and God Himself enters the stage and begins to speak. These are comforting words, effectively answering the prayer contained in the previous verses of the psalm. First, He promises His presence with His people in the church forever. This is His desire. These are beautiful words indeed: that God desires to be with His people. This was also the gist of the Abrahamic covenant. It's comforting to know that we are not asking Him to do something that He does not want to do. Our Lord Jesus chose twelve disciples to be "with Him" (Mark 3:14), and then promised He would be with them until the end of the age (Matt. 28:20). And finally, the entire plan is consummated at the end of time, when "God Himself shall be with them, and they shall be His people" (Rev. 21:3). He promises abundant physical and spiritual blessings to His people (verse 15). He answers the petition of verse nine with the promise of salvation for the priests, and joyful worship amongst the saints.

How do we apply this Psalm to our lives?

Whenever a family moves to a new geographical location, their number one priority (before finding their own home) should be to identify a good church with which to worship. The materialist age in which we live puts the job ahead of the church—or the school, the house, and the neighborhood ahead of the church. But the Christian would rather live in a tent in the wilderness with access to the assembly of true saints, than in some wealthy metropolitan area where there is no church with which to worship.

How does this Psalm teach us to worship God?

Our worship should be clothed in joy, with a true sense that Christ has secured the victory for us! The primary sentiment of worship is not sappy, flabby sentimentality or sadness. Nor is it a sharp angry tone, or a somber, prolonged gravity. While there may be a range of proper emotions expressed in worship, the preeminent emotion must an irrepressible, triumphant, loud-ringing joy. You will know that it is Christian church when you hear victorious shouts coming from the building in which the saints gather to worship!

Questions:

1. Where was David when he wrote this psalm? How far is this place from Jerusalem?

2. What is the state of Israel's worship assumed as the psalmist pens this psalm?

3. What are the two signs that the Spirit of God is within our assembly?

4. What happens to monarchies throughout the generations? Why is the Davidic monarchy so special?

5. What is the preeminent sentiment that should be present in God's worship?

Family Discussion Questions:

1. How do worship and the local church fit into our family's priorities? Would we move to a new area without the possibility of Christian worship?

2. Where is our joy in worship? Is our worship dull, somber, sentimental, or triumphant?

Psalm 133

Category: *Didactic*
Occasion: *Healthy Ecumenical Meetings*
Author: *David*

....

1 Behold, how good and how pleasant it is for brethren to dwell together in unity!
2 It is like the precious ointment upon the head, that ran down upon the beard, even Aaron's beard: that went down to the skirts of his garments;
3 As the dew of Hermon, and as the dew that descended upon the mountains of Zion: for there the Lord commanded the blessing, even life for evermore.

The Point:

Unity in the body of the church is a tremendous duty and blessing, because our God insists upon it.

How do we feel in the recitation of this Psalm?

There is something both delightful and refreshing about unity among brothers. When senseless divisions are removed and long-standing conflicts are resolved, unity breaks through and love wins. For example, most people delight in beautiful ambiance, romantic music, fine wine, and a sumptuous meal. These are considered the finer things of life. But God defines the finest of all delights—the unity of the church.

What does this Psalm say?

Verse 1

What are the best delights for God and man? What are the highest achievements a human can have on this earth? Only the right values can tell us the right answers to these questions, and only God Himself can establish these values. Man impresses himself with his towers, his military might, his wars won, and his technological developments. Henry Ford and Albert Einstein are heroes to many because they developed technology and military weaponry.

But what does God's Word define as the highest values of all? What is Jesus Christ's perspective on this? What was His primary prayer petition while He was here on earth? "I in them, and Thou in me, that they may be made perfect in one" (John 17:23). He repeats this petition three times in His wonderful prayer spoken at the end of His earthly ministry. Jesus loves oneness in His body. He desires it. He preaches it, prays for it, and nurtures it.

In a world where the Arabs and Jews have been arch-enemies for 4,000 years, and wars continue without respite everywhere, we all understand the magnitude of the challenges. Wars, disunity, and fracturing characterize this world. But it must not be so with Christ and His church. Within the organized church, disunity does appear from time to time, but there is a purpose for it. "There must be factions among you in order that those who are genuine among you may be recognized" (1 Cor. 11:19). Where there are schisms, it is to prove that which is authentic. That which remains orthodox and faith-filled through the storms of apostasy proves itself tried and true. Major denominations break from the historical and biblical church perspective on the Trinity, or on homosexuality, and they prove themselves to be schismatic. Sometimes orthodox, biblical churches find schisms within their ranks because of pride and undue focus on questionable doctrines and "strifes of words" (1 Tim. 1:4, 6:4).

Truly, sustained unity among men is a supernatural thing. It is a refreshing, beautiful reality in the Church of Jesus Christ. If there is restored relationship and peace between a holy God and the believer, there had better be some reflection of that between believers.

If church-going professing Christians have lost the unity between themselves entirely and all is unreconciled, then they must still need to be reconciled with God. If they have no love of the brethren, the love of God must not reside in them (1 John 4:20). Thus, the miracle of Christ's reconciling work must be witnessed first and foremost within the body of the church. Nothing on earth is of higher value than the love between brethren. David and Jonathan seem to have experienced it a bit (1 Sam. 18). Within the Church established by Jesus Christ, friendship and unity should be normative, a tremendous testimony to the world around us.

Verses 2-3

Two analogies are used in these verses to help us understand the beauty of true biblical unity. It is like precious ointment poured on Aaron's head at his installation as High Priest in Israel (Exod. 29:7, 30:23, Lev. 18:12). Like fragrant oil that creates an extremely pleasant and peaceful atmosphere, unity between brothers and sisters in the church makes the church a comfortable and attractive place to be. Disunity in the church, especially among the leadership, results in extreme discomfort, loss, pain, spiritual decay, and sometimes the collapse of entire churches.

The second analogy describes unity between brothers as something like the spring of life. Without the dew from the heavens watering the earth, no vegetation will ever grow (Deut. 33:28). That's what distinguishes the green covered hills of Zion from the desert. Typically, water runoff from the highest mountains (such as Mount Hermon at 9,230 ft.), served as a major source of irrigation for the fields and hills below. Without unity in the body, we will have dried up fields, withered fruit, and a languishing kingdom work. May God give us this blessing of unity in rich abundance, here and now! When the early church gathered with one accord, with a unified faith in the risen Christ, the Spirit of God came upon them and filled the place with His power (Acts 2:1ff). Unity is the precursor to powerful work in the church of our Lord Jesus Christ.

Not only does our Lord Jesus Christ desire the blessing of unity, He commands it. It is more than a directive. It is a certain reality, because He will ordain that unity. One way or another, He will bring it to pass in Zion. You can count on it. Of course, He may bring it about through persecution, trials, and by pruning the vine. Our local churches may face obstacles along the way, such as false brothers, divisive factions, and heretical schisms. But, mark these words well. Our Lord commands the blessing and He will have it.

How do we apply this Psalm to our lives?

Let us appreciate unity and seek unity in the church body. We ought to strive to keep the unity of the Spirit in the bond of peace (Eph. 4:3). This may come about by humbling ourselves, confessing our sins, and sacrificing our own pride and comforts in the process. We may need to go the extra mile to open up communication channels and resolve conflicts with our brothers and sisters. Unity 101 happens within the Christian family. Whenever there are offenses, we should be quick to confess our own sins, and even quicker to forgive one another.

How does this Psalm teach us to worship God?

Corporate worship is based upon love for one another, and a unified confession. We have the greatest basis for unity on earth, because we know that we are undeserving, wretched sinners who have all been wonderfully saved by the same Savior.

We ought to have a special appreciation for the gifts that the Spirit of God pours out upon Aaron, and any other person who ministers in the church. To despise prophesying or any other gift in the church is to despise the Spirit who is the Giver of these gifts (1 Thess. 5:20). When we are despising the preaching, the prayers, or any other contribution to the church, we quench the Spirit of God. Why should He pour out any more gifts upon a congregation that despises the gifts He has already given? The oil pouring off of Aaron's head represents the unity of the Spirit in the bond of peace (Eph. 4:1-3). This unity is complemented by a multiplicity of gifts that comes from the outpouring of the Spirit of God upon the church.

Questions:

1. What does Jesus pray for in His pastoral prayer in John 17?

2. What does the picture of oil running down Aaron's beard signify?

3. Where in the Old Testament do we find brothers in unity with one another? Provide at least one example.

4. What does the picture of the dew from Hermon signify?

5. How does Christ bring about unity in His churches?

Family Discussion Questions:

1. What are the things that create disunity in the church? Have we witnessed any of these things?

2. Do we appreciate the gifts that God has given our church? Who has been sharing gifts lately in our church, and how can we appreciate them?

PSALM 134

Category: *Ascent, Praise*
Occasion: *A Short Church Service*
Author: *Unknown*

....

1 Behold, bless ye the Lord, all ye servants of the Lord, which by
   night stand in the house of the Lord.
2 Lift up your hands in the sanctuary, and bless the Lord.
3 The Lord that made heaven and earth bless thee out of Zion.

The Point:

We bless God above, and at the same time we pray God's blessing
on one another.

How do we feel in the recitation of this Psalm?

Our hearts are filled to the brim with warm, grateful, and glorious consideration of God in our worship. This naturally moves into
gracious, kind, and appreciative consideration of our brothers and
sisters in Christ who worship with us in the same body.

What does this Psalm say?

Verse 1

In this last ascent psalm, it is as though we have finally ascended the
hill and have arrived at the worship service itself. This little psalm

nicely encapsulates the worship service in three verses. While the service must include both the vertical (worship of God), and horizontal (edification of the brothers and sisters), we must begin in the vertical. Loving God is the first commandment, and then we love our neighbor. We will never love our neighbor in the true sense of the word, if we cannot first love God. And, as John puts it, we love Him because He first loved us (1 John. 4:17). When we truly comprehend His love for us, we will love Him and then we will love others too. This is the basis for the worship service.

We begin the psalm by calling out to our brothers, fellow servants of Christ, to worship Him and bless Him. The Hebrew word used for bless (*barak*) combines sincere reverence with appreciatory words of praise. As was Moses at the burning bush, we are sensitive to the fact that we stand on holy ground. We are aware of the grand majesty, the white-hot holiness, the sovereign power, and piercing omniscience of the God whom we worship. This must affect our demeanor and posture in worship. But then, we want to express words of favorable sentiments and praise to our Lord. We have been the recipients of His grace and kindness. We have witnessed works of power, judgment, and overwhelming mercy. We have narrowly escaped the clutches of evil by His grace, and we cannot help but praise our Lord. In fact, the longer we live, the more we have to say of His truth, His salvation, and His sovereign rule.

Praise and worship is hardly an occasional activity for the believer. Modern Western Christians have grown unaccustomed to daily worship, but this is a common pattern in places where the Church is healthy and growing. Daily worship services, sometimes twice daily, sometimes exceeding an hour or two per service, were not unusual in the history of the Church. Christians stand up to worship God by night because they desire it. Better is a day in your courts, than a thousand elsewhere! (Ps. 84:10).

Verse 2

There are comparatively few specific directions given for our worship in Scripture, but here is one. Must we always leave our hands hanging down at our side. or stuck in our pockets when we worship, or folded in the expression of modern piety? When a church no longer engages robust worship, in the lifting up of hearts, voices, and hands, there must be some anemia setting in to that body. Both the Old and New Testament command the lifting up of the hands for praise and worship (ref. 1 Tim. 2:8). The New Testament injunction calls on men to lead in prayer (and the raising of the hands), but this does not restrict women from the practice. John Calvin certifies that this was the practice of the church through the ages. He writes in his commentary on 1 Timothy 2, "This attitude has been generally used in worship during all ages; for it is a feeling which nature has implanted in us." Of course, the frequency and specific method are not ordered here, and should be left to individuals and particular gatherings of the saints. Fervent men and women will use their hands in worship—that is the plain and simple truth of it. However, all singing, all kneeling, all praying, and all hand-raising can be faked. Worship is always a matter of the heart. If the heart and mind are not committed to the worship of God, all the rituals, confessions, and psalm-singing become empty externals. May God rid us of all hypocrisy and formalism in our worship, and give us hearts full of praise for our God.

Verse 3

While the first two verses speak of our praise to God, here the psalm moves towards the horizontal. This is the order of every one of our public worship services. First we bless God, and then we ask for God's blessing on His people. We look around us and see our brothers and sisters in the Lord, and we say, "God, please bless these people!"

Nobody has the capability or the goodness to bless us more than the Creator of heaven and earth. If He has already provided us with all of the resources in the universe, of course He can bless His people out of Zion. The blessings flow out of Zion, because the church is the object of His love. The Son of God gave His life for the church, and He is "head of all things to the church" (Eph. 1:22). His blessings flow from His church.

How do we apply this Psalm to our lives?

We are the servants of God, and we owe Him our allegiance day by day. We are not our own, for we are bought with a price (1 Cor.

6:20). Every day when we get out of bed, we must remember that we are here to do service for the Lord Jesus Christ. When we lift our hands to our God, we are telling Him that we are His servants and we offer our lives to His service.

How does this Psalm teach us to worship God?

Our worship service must be one continuous blessing. First and foremost, our worship is directed in the vertical as we praise God together. It is blessing God by telling God how blessed He is, and then declaring and petitioning God's blessing upon His people.

Questions:

1. What are the two blessings offered in this psalm?

2. What is a blessing, as described by the Hebrew word?

3. What are we saying when we lift our hands in worship?

Family Discussion Questions:

1. Would you classify our worship services as warm, grateful, and glorious? Is this a regular or an occasional occurrence?

2. What are some of the reasons that we want to bless God?

3. Do we lift our voices, hearts, and hands in worship? Why or why not?

PSALM 135

Category: *Praise*
Occasion: *Casting Down Idols*
Author: *Unknown*

....

1 Praise ye the Lord. Praise ye the name of the Lord; praise Him, O ye servants of the Lord.

2 Ye that stand in the house of the Lord, in the courts of the house of our God.

3 Praise the Lord; for the Lord is good: sing praises unto His name; for it is pleasant.

4 For the Lord hath chosen Jacob unto himself, and Israel for his peculiar treasure.

5 For I know that the Lord is great, and that our Lord is above all gods.

6 Whatsoever the Lord pleased, that did He in heaven, and in earth, in the seas, and all deep places.

7 He causeth the vapours to ascend from the ends of the earth; he maketh lightnings for the rain; he bringeth the wind out of His treasuries.

8 Who smote the firstborn of Egypt, both of man and beast.

9 Who sent tokens and wonders into the midst of thee, O Egypt, upon Pharaoh, and upon all his servants.

10 Who smote great nations, and slew mighty kings;

11 Sihon king of the Amorites, and Og king of Bashan, and all the kingdoms of Canaan:

12 And gave their land for an heritage, an heritage unto Israel His

people.

13 Thy name, O Lord, endureth for ever; and thy memorial, O Lord, throughout all generations.

14 For the Lord will judge His people, and He will repent himself concerning His servants.

15 The idols of the heathen are silver and gold, the work of men's hands.

16 They have mouths, but they speak not; eyes have they, but they see not;

17 They have ears, but they hear not; neither is there any breath in their mouths.

18 They that make them are like unto them: so is every one that trusteth in them.

19 Bless the Lord, O house of Israel: bless the Lord, O house of Aaron:

20 Bless the Lord, O house of Levi: ye that fear the Lord, bless the Lord.

21 Blessed be the Lord out of Zion, which dwelleth at Jerusalem. Praise ye the Lord.

The Point:

The gods of the heathen and the humanists are all ridiculous idols, and only the sovereign God over heaven and earth is worth worshiping.

How do we feel in the recitation of this Psalm?

There is nothing more delightful than to gather with the saints and lift praises to our God. All other worship is profoundly unsatisfying and vain. In our worship, we will boast in the works of the true and living God and mock the gods of the heathen.

What does this Psalm say?

Verses 1–3

Some psalms dedicate themselves almost entirely to the praise of God, and this is one of them. Repeatedly, the psalmist exhorts us to praise God. When we say these words with the psalmist, we are instructing ourselves and every person to lift praises to our God.

The psalm is captured by two bookends, instructions to praise at the beginning and more instructions to praise and bless the Lord at the end. These words are best shouted out to the entire assembly, because the goal is to see that everybody joins in. It is directed towards those who are servants of the Lord, and those who stand in the house of God. Too much worship is performed while sitting today, and this may be another sign of anemia and irreverence. If our hearts are thinking reverently, we will want to express that reverence by standing—or kneeling—either way. These are the natural expressions of the heart. If we are standing out of rote ritualism, and if our thoughts are anything but Godward, then we have fake reverence and it is worth nothing.

The praise described in this psalm is pleasant. There is something satisfying in work, because we are created to work. But there is something even more satisfying in worship—it is the highest endeavor in all of human existence. The dung beetle is created to consume dung, and the vulture is created to clean up carrion, but the human is created for a wholly different purpose. When men dedicate their lives to self-consumption, idolatries, and degrading sexual practices, they act the part of the dung beetle instead of the part of the human made in the image of God. When we finally make it to the congregation of the saints and our minds soar with meditations on the holiness, majesty, and love of God, we have achieved the ultimate purpose of our creation. We take to the heavens like the bird who knows how to use his wings and fulfill his Creator's intent for him.

Verses 4–7

These verses present the overarching theme of the psalm, offering two prime reasons for praising God. First, we praise God because He has chosen us as His peculiar people (1 Pet. 2:9). He has "chosen us that [we] should show forth the praises of Him who hath called us out of darkness into His marvelous light!" Secondly, we laud His Name for His greatness and His transcendence above all other gods. This becomes the theme for the rest of the psalm. It is crucial that we know God's authority over all of the gods of the earth. Either these are authorities among men, powerful institutions within the created world, or they are false gods constructed in the imaginations of the hearts of men. Whatever the case, we must be absolutely convinced in our minds that God is the absolute sovereign over all.

Look up and take in everything around you, and then consider that these are all the purposes of God in action. He is accomplishing His will everywhere. The dew that falls gently on the earth and the violent storms are all according to His plans. He has ordered our days. He arranges the weather patterns, the sentient life, the birds flying through the air, the microbes that introduce disease to the body, and the powers of government. The same thing can be said of the storms on Jupiter that have been raging for hundreds of years. The storm seen from our planet as the eye of Jupiter is the size of our globe, and would wipe out all life on Earth in ten minutes. God does whatever He wants to do, and there is no force greater than He that can overrule His purposes. Thus, we conclude that the Creator of Heaven and Earth is the One who is ultimately qualified to receive our worship.

Verses 8-14

This next portion of the psalm speaks to God's supremacy over the great empires of the earth. Sometimes man will attempt to compete with God for His worship. After all, man has intelligence and assumes authority over his fellow creatures. Man was created for dominion over the fish of the sea and the fowl of the air (Ps. 8:6-8). Initially intended to act as God's vice-regent on the earth, man revolted against God, formed his own kingdoms, and began to tyrannize his fellow men. God does not allow this to continue indefinitely, however. He brings these rebellious kingdoms down. Most spectacularly, He brought the great Egyptian empire down at the Red Sea. He did this in order that He might save His people and establish His own kingdom. Old Testament Israel was only a microcosm of God's program on earth. Throughout history, He continues to bring the kingdoms of men down, while preserving His own people in the process.

Verses 15-18

There are only two types of gods that attempt to displace the true God in the mind of man and compete for his worship. Humanist man presents himself as god, and attempts to usurp God's worship. That was the subject of verses 8-14. Then there is the god that men create in the imagination of their hearts. In this section, the psalmist goes after these false gods, contrasting them with the true and living God. Baal, Ashteroth, Pele, and a thousand other gods have faded away, but Jehovah God is still served and worshipped by His people 6,000 years later. Of course, the gods that are formed by men's hands and imaginations are ridiculous gods. It is all a farce and a pretense, though not many idolaters would want to admit to it. Why would the creator of a god fall down on his face and worship the god he just created? These gods are very important to the idolators, but they have not created heaven and earth. They are not sovereign over the entire universe. Materialists worship their houses and cars (which they have built for themselves), but these creations are less impressive than the men who created them. They have no arms or legs. They cannot reason. Their mechanical parts cannot repair themselves, as in the case of man's cellular systems. Unless men constantly maintain and repair these gods, they will deteriorate over time. What a contrast with the true and living God who Himself providentially sustains His whole creation and who endures forever!

Verses 19-21

These three verses constitute the second bookend of the psalm. The first three verses open with instructions to praise God, and now the psalm ends with instructions to bless Him. The Hebrew word for "praise," (*halal*) connotes a glorious, exalting boasting performed in the standing position, while the word for "bless," (*barak*) you will remember represents more of a humble, warm, adoration often expressed in the kneeling position.

How do we apply this Psalm to our lives?

Let us submit to God's authority, first, by refusing to create any other gods or give any credence to any other gods at the expense of the true and living God.

Let us also express reverence to God—by kneeling, lifting our hands, or standing in worship. When we mumble our prayers in a half-hearted or rote manner, we act as if we are speaking to a God who is hardly God, or a God whom we hardly believe exists. First, let us identify the God we worship and then let us appeal to Him as if He is that God.

How does this Psalm teach us to worship God?

In our worship, we must set aside all of the other concerns that battle for our attention. These are competing gods, and they must be cast aside if we are to worship the true and living God. This includes our concern for our health, our lives, our children, our wealth, and indeed even our own spouses.

Questions:

1. What are the bookends to the psalm? What is the difference between the words "praise" and "bless"?

2. Why is worship pleasant to us?

3. What are the two types of gods that compete for our attention, mentioned in this psalm?

4. How does Jehovah God differ from the old gods of the heathen?

5. Why must we consider it so ridiculous that people turn their material possessions (as in cars or houses) into their gods?

Family Discussion Questions:

1. Are there any gods that compete for our attention and worship? How might we correct our thinking about these gods? How do we speak and how should we speak about these false gods?

2. How much do you reverence God in your worship? When you stand before God or kneel before Him, are you expressing your humble service to the Lord Jesus Christ?

PSALM 136

Category: *Thanksgiving*
Occasion: *Remembrance of God's Temporal and Eternal Blessings*
Author: *Unknown*

....

1   O give thanks unto the Lord; for He is good: for His mercy endureth for ever.
2   O give thanks unto the God of gods: for His mercy endureth for ever.
3   O give thanks to the Lord of lords: for His mercy endureth for ever.
4   To Him who alone doeth great wonders: for His mercy endureth for ever.
5   To Him that by wisdom made the heavens: for His mercy endureth for ever.
6   To Him that stretched out the earth above the waters: for His mercy endureth for ever.
7   To Him that made great lights: for His mercy endureth for ever:
8   The sun to rule by day: for His mercy endureth for ever:
9   The moon and stars to rule by night: for His mercy endureth for ever.
10 To Him that smote Egypt in their firstborn: for His mercy endureth for ever:
11 And brought out Israel from among them: for His mercy endureth for ever:
12 With a strong hand, and with a stretched out arm: for His mercy endureth for ever.
13 To Him which divided the Red Sea into parts: for His mercy endureth for ever:
14 And made Israel to pass through the midst of it: for His mercy

endureth for ever:

15 But overthrew Pharaoh and his host in the Red sea: for His mercy endureth for ever.

16 To Him which led his people through the wilderness: for His mercy endureth for ever.

17 To Him which smote great kings: for His mercy endureth for ever:

18 And slew famous kings: for His mercy endureth for ever:

19 Sihon king of the Amorites: for His mercy endureth for ever:

20 And Og the king of Bashan: for His mercy endureth for ever:

21 And gave their land for an heritage: for His mercy endureth for ever:

22 Even an heritage unto Israel His servant: for His mercy endureth for ever.

23 Who remembered us in our low estate: for His mercy endureth for ever:

24 And hath redeemed us from our enemies: for His mercy endureth for ever.

25 Who giveth food to all flesh: for His mercy endureth for ever.

26 O give thanks unto the God of heaven: for His mercy endureth for ever.

The Point:

God's love and mercy towards His people will endure forever.

How do we feel in the recitation of this Psalm?

The point is driven home again and again. It is impossible to miss the message. Repetition provides emphasis, and when a thought is repeated 26 times in a single psalm, we cannot help but fixate upon the point. When we are told that God's love and tender mercy towards us has no ending, all of our doubts, fears, and insecurities evaporate instantly. If we were to picture it in human terms, it is more the love of a husband who would care for his invalid wife for forty years, rather than some temporary romantic fling. It is a love that conquers life and death, all principality and power, though all hell assail it. It is a love that truly never fails. If we are sure of anything that God reveals to us in His Word, we are sure of this. We feel completely secure in the love of God as we read this psalm, and we offer warm thanksgivings for all of His benefits.

What does this Psalm say?

Verses 1-3

This is the great presupposition that we take to our knees before we open our mouths in prayer. God is good. If God were not good, then why would we bother with prayer at all? We give thanks to God because He is good. Those who have denied the faith and embraced atheism typically start down that path by rejecting the goodness of God as the great basic proposition of their lives. They presume their own goodness and reject God's goodness.

The goodness of God should be the fundamental characteristic of our outlook on our entire life. We open our eyes and see His goodness everywhere. The goodness of God rushes into our consciousness. God is good despite the sin of man and the destruction that attends man's wretched rebellion. His goodness is seen in His eternal mercy demonstrated towards His people. Sometimes we call this His "covenant mercies." The tender mercies of the wicked are cruel (Prov. 12:10), and the mercies of our closest friends will often come to an end after a year or two. But the mercies of God never run out. They continue from one generation to the next and then on into eternity. Perhaps after a million years in eternity we will better understand the unfailing, eternal nature of God's mercies—but we will never entirely comprehend it.

Verses two and three acknowledge His great authority over all authorities. He is God over all gods/authorities and Lord over all lords. We understand the concept of human authority, and we typically respect its offices. If we have no respect for our civil government, we will be quickly overcome by it. Nonetheless, the source of all good things is God. So, when lower authorities (humans and devils) exercise evil upon the earth, God will turn these things to good. This also provides reason to praise Him! He can and will turn all things to good and to His own glory, precisely because He is the ultimate sovereign.

Therefore, we praise Him, and we thank Him. As far as we can see the good He has done in the world, we must thank Him for it. At each point that we recognize God's redemption, God's gifts, and God's goodness in creation and providence, we must offer our sacrifices of praise and thanksgiving to Him. When we cease to offer these sacrifices, we are failing to recognize the gifts themselves as well as the Giver.

Verses 4-9

These verses speak of God's mighty work of creation. He alone does great wonders. Yes, humans can manufacture buildings and jet airplanes, but these do not come close to meeting the criteria of "great wonders." Powerful earthquakes and hurricanes can destroy men's greatest achievements in mere seconds. Whatever men produce is only a derivative of God's original creation. What then does His mercy have to do with His powerful creative works? Our minds cannot comprehend eternal mercies, because, among mere mortals, we have not encountered anybody who can guarantee mercy for more than a day or two. If God, however, can make a universe of stars in a place where it takes billions of years for light to travel from one side to the other, then naturally He is big enough to guarantee mercy to those who receive His promise. These heavenly bodies also testify to His long-standing faithfulness. Human beneficence runs out quickly. Occasionally, a gift lasts for thirty or forty years. But God's gifts of the sun, the moon, and stars continue to shine on this earth for at least six thousand years, without failing.

We must remember that this is a thanksgiving psalm. Since our God made the heavens, and His mercy is magnificent and unending, let us give thanks to Him!

Verses 10-22

This section moves into the great redemptive story of the Old Testament, when the Lord delivered His people out of Egypt. In all of the records of history, there has never been such a story of physical deliverance like this one. Never was an empire and its vast armies destroyed so suddenly, and a weak and enslaved people delivered by such a magnificent demonstration of power. This is how God holds true to His covenant promises to Abraham many years earlier. The Israelites who recited this psalm in 800 BC would reflect on God's covenant mercies extending four hundred years between the promise given to Abraham and the deliverance from Egypt. Then again, His mercies extended another forty years while the children of Israel wandered in the wilderness. Then, these mercies of God extended another 600 years through the period of the judges and the kings, as God provided a temporal fulfillment of His promise to Abraham (in the provision of the land). They would have to wait another 800 years before God's people would see a fulfillment of His covenant mercies to His people in the form of David's Son, Jesus Christ, and the rightful King of Israel.

Verses 23-26

These final words encapsulate the message of redemption. Why this redemption story? Why does God order such dreadful conditions and this dramatic rescue? Of course, it is one unforgettable object lesson that points to something far more important in my life and yours. All of us are enslaved under more horrific conditions than what we find with Israel in Egypt. By nature, we are all enslaved to sin and the devil. And Jesus Christ, the very Son of God, comes to us in our low condition and delivers us in a more spectacular redemption than that performed at the Red Sea. And though we may be halfway out of Egypt, halfway across the Red Sea, or halfway across the Desert of Sinai, we are assured that He is delivering us out of the hands of our enemies. His mercies will go the distance. His mercies really do endure forever.

Verse 25 is an unusual addition, almost a non sequitur in the proceedings of the psalm. This verse mentions God's feeding of the animals. We know that humans take care of several billion domesticated animals around the globe, but Yahweh God cares for several quadrillion insects, fish, birds, and wild beasts in the oceans and fields from Antarctica to the Arctic, from the Sahara Desert to the Tibetan mountains. How is this comforting to us? In the words of our Lord, if our heavenly Father cares for the birds of the air and the lilies in the field, He will much more attend to our needs as well. "Are you not of more value than they?" (Matt. 6:26)

How do we apply this Psalm to our lives?

Much of this psalm deals with the violent destruction of great and powerful kings for the benefit of God's people. We must apply these Old Testament metaphors to the violent destructive work Christ has done for us against sin and the devil. The language used in the New Testament concerning this spiritual warfare is intensely violent. The Lord Jesus Christ destroys the one who holds the power of death and condemns him to eternal hell fire (Heb. 2:14). He treads the winepress of the wrath of almighty God and smites the nations (Rev. 19:15). He triumphs over principalities and powers at the cross (Col. 2:15). Our response must be great and mighty cheers for the conquering work of our Savior-King! From the perspective of the new man in Christ, we delight to see the flesh, the world, and the devil taking devastating blows from the hand of our Lord.

How does this Psalm teach us to worship God?

- Very few of the inspired songs in the Word of God provide choruses and repetition. In fact, our Lord Jesus Christ warns us against using vain repetition as the heathen do (Matt. 6:7). Nonetheless, occasional choruses may be used for the sake of emphasis. When worship is nothing but repetition, the things that really ought to be emphasized can be lost in the cacophony. Let us make selective use of repetition, as we find in the book of Psalms.

- The story of redemption in the Old Testament is our story as well. As we view the dead, bloated bodies of Pharaoh's army washing up on the shore, we are reminded of the work that Christ has done for us. There can be no redemption without the destruction of our enemies. Put yourself in the story of the Red Sea and experience the great relief, the sense of victory, the breathtaking power of God, and the joy of deliverance felt on that great day.

- Our worship and prayer must always include an element of thanksgiving. "Be careful for nothing; but in every thing by prayer and supplication with thanksgiving let your requests be made known unto God" (Phil. 4:6). In our thanksgivings, let us reflect upon the essential goodness of God that is the source of every good and gracious gift.

Questions:

1. How does God's mighty creation buttress our faith in His everlasting mercy?

2. What was the temporal fulfillment of God's promise to Abraham? What was the final fulfillment of that promise to Abraham?

3. At what point does God come to deliver us, according to verse 23?

4. How does the Bible handle repetition in psalms (songs)? What does our Lord Jesus Christ say about the use of repetition?

5. How many animals does God feed around the world? How does God's providential care for His creatures encourage us, His children?

Family Discussion Questions:

1. How often do our prayers and worship reflect thankfulness to God? Do we tend to move straight to the petition and forget the manifold blessings God has poured out upon us?

2. Let us recount God's goodness to us right here and now. What are the blessings you can see, hear, and remember?

PSALM 137

Category: *Imprecatory*
Occasion: *A Decimated Church*
Author: *Unknown*

....

1 By the rivers of Babylon, there we sat down, yea, we wept, when we remembered Zion.
2 We hanged our harps upon the willows in the midst thereof.
3 For there they that carried us away captive required of us a song; and they that wasted us required of us mirth, saying, Sing us one of the songs of Zion.
4 How shall we sing the Lord's song in a strange land?
5 If I forget thee, O Jerusalem, let my right hand forget her cunning.
6 If I do not remember thee, let my tongue cleave to the roof of my mouth; if I prefer not Jerusalem above my chief joy.
7 Remember, O Lord, the children of Edom in the day of Jerusalem; who said, Rase it, rase it, even to the foundation thereof.
8 O daughter of Babylon, who art to be destroyed; happy shall he be, that rewardeth thee as thou hast served us.
9 Happy shall he be, that taketh and dasheth thy little ones against the stones.

The Point:

God will destroy every kingdom on earth before He will permit the obliteration of His people.

How do we feel in the recitation of this Psalm?

Scandals. Schisms. Persecutions. Satanic Attacks. Practically everyday, these things threaten to blow the church into a million bits. Almost every local church will face this scenario at some point-in the day they take that very serious hit. The hand grenade rolls (in a metaphoric sense), and the entire body is shattered by some horrible scandal. Or, there is a gradual decline into utter spiritual bankruptcy. Meantime, the enemies of the church screech in morbid delight and mocking scorn. So there the remainder of the church sits in a stunned malaise, and the only psalm left to sing is this one. It is hardly a song, more a dirge. The sentiment is pure, embittered grief expressed over the condition of the church of the Lord Jesus Christ. Any true Christian facing the severe apostasy of the Western church led by Rome in the 1480s, or the apostasy of the English church in the 1950s, or the apostasy of the American church in the 2010s would have resonated to this psalm with every fiber of his being. This psalm may apply to a local church situation or to a very large and severe breakdown of an entire faith community.

What does this Psalm say?

Verse 1-4

Following severe spiritual decline, God's people find themselves in exile under the persecuting hand of cruel pagans. They find themselves without material sustenance, spiritual vitality, political influence, or a cultural integrity. Their children seem to be absorbing into the ways of the pagans, by way of their educational and cultural programs. It is a far cry from the glory days of the Davidic kingdom. For the modern Christian, we have come a very long way from the glory days of the 16th-century Reformation. What is described here is the worst of all worlds from the perspective of the lone believer here and there. From this vantage point, there appears to be little hope that God's people will survive on planet earth.

The captors seem to be taunting the people of God, asking them for a song. Now that the true faith is "destroyed" and the church is considered completely irrelevant, the world invites us to the last thing to do—join in with the worldly mirth. The world cannot understand why we mourn. While the world is celebrating gay pride, God's people are mourning, they are humbled and impoverished of spirit (Matt. 5:3ff). We are cast down as we see our own sin and the abject brokenness of the church. When we catch a vision for the true state of things at a time when the church is best described as wretched, poor, blind, and naked (Rev. 3:18), then we cry out for God's mercy. We have no time for gay celebrations and proud festivals while what is needed most is sackcloth and ashes. The world revels in its sins, and cannot see the body is full of sores from head to toe (Isa. 1:6). They carve happy faces into the open sores, and heal the wounds so slightly (Jer. 6:14). Meanwhile God's people cannot help but face the painful realities in the present, and they mourn. They mourn the compromise, the weakness, the disunity, the rebellion, the generational apostasy, the worldliness, the persecution from the world, the scandals, the breakdown of faith, the paucity of shepherds, the total absence of any spiritual revival, the depression and psychological torments, the excommunications, the laxity in church discipline, internal treachery, church splits, the rarity of love and peace between brothers, and a hundred other maladies in the church. The world looks at us and laughs, but we will mourn.

Verses 5-6

These verses confirm the tremendous value we place upon the church of God. When every one of our friends are disillusioned and jaded by the hypocrisy, the insincerity, the inner turmoil, the church splits, the scandals; and when theological systems are undermining the importance of the visible church everywhere, we will never give up on the body of Christ. Though our hands may lose their functions and cannot play the instruments, and though our voices be incapable of forming a syllable, we will prefer Jerusalem as our chief joy. True, we may not realize the joy of the church at this moment in history while we sit in exile, as we watch the enemy do its worst to the unity and integrity of the body. We rather feel sorrow, pity, and a holy indignation at the plight of God's people. Nevertheless, we are still holding out for our highest joy and expectation—the assembly of genuine faith in relationship with the living Christ, the true manifestation of the love of God in the Christian brotherhood, and the joy that comes with the communion of the Holy Spirit. Though we may only experience this imperfectly here on earth, one day we will see the perfect consummation of this vision in the heavenly Jerusalem.

Verses 7-9

Now, the psalmist turns his attention to the enemies of the people of God. Primarily, these enemies appear for us in the form of the world, the flesh, and the devil. The church has always had its enemies. From the beginning, Israel was tormented by the Edomites (or the descendants of Esau). It was more than a cultural (or "racial") difference. The Edomites despised the covenant promises of God and thereby set themselves as arch-enemies of God Himself. When the church faces persecution from the world, they must know that the deep-seated enmity is set against the Creator and their lawful King. That is why Edom is so keen on the utter destruction of Jerusalem.

Now come some of the most bitter language ever uttered in inspired writings (vs. 8,9). Before rushing to judgment, however, one must be careful not to misinterpret what is being said. Israel's enemy is Babylon who has brought God's people into exile. However, it has already been prophesied that this heathen nation will be conquered by King Cyrus of the Medo-Persian empire. With that in mind, the psalmist says, Happy shall these Persians be to take the Babylonian babies and dash their heads against a stone." Strong words indeed, but it is important to recognize what is not being said. Certainly, the psalmist is not claiming this "rejoicing" for himself or for any of God's people. It will be the enemies of the Babylonians that will be happy to destroy the Babylonians—man, woman, and child. This simply certifies the certainty of the destruction of the Babylonian power, and the tragic nature of that terrible fate. Although God's people may falter into hypocrisy, synthesis with the world, and ignominy, any and all who lift a finger against the church may be sure they will never get away with it.

How do we apply this Psalm to our lives?

Many of us who live in the Western world have experienced something of these sentiments over the last 75 years or so. We have felt the grief of a tattered and torn church amid the elation of the atheists, the humanists, and the progressives who have moved in to dominate the educational, political, and cultural institutions of the day. They call us out to the streets to sing a few carols on Christmas Eve, and they ignore us the rest of the year.

If the church is our chief joy and our primary commitment, then we ought to mourn a little for the way it is treated in our day. Church discipline is often disregarded. Pastors are a despised class, and Sunday preaching bears a fraction of the influence on the congregants as do the movies they watch on Saturday night. What a tragic condition for what is supposed to be the very body and bride of Christ! Only one who deeply values the body of Christ can sing a psalm like this with true sentiment. May God help all of us to greatly value the church of the Lord Jesus Christ (who loved that church and gave Himself for it).

How does this Psalm teach us to worship God?

These imprecatory psalms introduce a very different sentiment into the church. It is a love for the church that yields hatred and bitterness towards that which destroys the church. Should a husband not wish to protect his bride as he watches her being beaten by some hoodlum with a baseball bat, we would be concerned for his apathy. Wouldn't we expect a violent, jealous reaction if his wife were subjected to such cruel treatment? Let us reintroduce these biblical sentiments back into worship.

Questions:

1. What is the setting for this psalm?

2. Why are God's people reticent to sing a song of Zion? What are they doing instead?

3. Why does Edom want to see the destruction of the people of God?

4. What nation will come to punish the "Daughter of Babylon?" What will this nation do to the small children of Babylon?

5. What are the primary enemies to the church today?

Family Discussion Questions:

1. Why would we sing a psalm like this one in the same spirit in which the psalmist expresses himself?

2. What is our chief joy or the things we value most on this earth?

Psalm 138

Category: *Praise*
Occasion: *Trouble on Every Side*
Author: *David*

....

1 I will praise thee with my whole heart: before the gods will I sing praise unto thee.

2 I will worship toward thy holy temple, and praise thy name for thy lovingkindness and for thy truth: for thou hast magnified thy word above all thy name.

3 In the day when I cried thou answeredst me, and strengthenedst me with strength in my soul.

4 All the kings of the earth shall praise thee, O Lord, when they hear the words of thy mouth.

5 Yea, they shall sing in the ways of the Lord: for great is the glory of the Lord.

6 Though the Lord be high, yet hath he respect unto the lowly: but the proud he knoweth afar off.

7 Though I walk in the midst of trouble, thou wilt revive me: thou shalt stretch forth thine hand against the wrath of mine enemies, and thy right hand shall save me.

8 The Lord will perfect that which concerneth me: thy mercy, O Lord, endureth for ever: forsake not the works of thine own hands.

The Point:

Though surrounded by trouble, the psalmist will still praise God and hope in God's final success with His Kingdom work.

How do we feel in the recitation of this Psalm?

Imagine the sentiment of the Christian who sits in a communist prison somewhere under the absolute control of cruel tyrants. When facing serious troubles like this, we learn that we are actually very small people, each of us. As we confront enemies larger than us, overwhelmed by troubles on every side, we become more intimately aware of our smallness and weakness. However, it is just when we discover our smallness, that we learn to glory in the bigness of God. This psalm demonstrates the right response to serious trouble. We summon the boldness to call upon the most powerful forces on earth to glorify God, and then we become oblivious to the threats of the enemy. Towards the end of the psalm, we gain more confidence that God will intervene for us and save us despite the attacks of the enemy.

What does this Psalm say?

Verses 1-2

The corporate officers frowned on the Christian as he breathed out a prayer of praise, "Praise be to the Lord!" The university professor mocked the student who said, "Thank you, Jesus!" when he received his graded exam. And the pastor was taken away in handcuffs when he tried to pray in the name of Christ before the nation's Supreme Court. Whether or not these words of praise to God are received, the psalmist is determined to praise Him anyway before the highest authorities (the gods) of the earth. Given that God is above all and worthy of our praise, the Christian cannot possibly render more recognition to the authorities of the earth than he does to God. He cannot but offer praise and worship to God with his whole heart. Truly, any God-fearing believer in Jesus Christ should never think twice of praising God in the presence of the most powerful men on earth. And it is no disrespect for these authorities, for no authority has any authority unless derived from God Himself (Rom. 13:1).

We worship God when we are confronted by His grace and truth (vs. 2). Without these two elements, we could not possibly relate to God. If it were only His truth, we would be undone and condemned forever; and if it were only His grace, we would never know the way to God and we would still be lost in deceit and sinful living. Importantly for us, both grace and truth came by Jesus Christ in the fullest possible sense (John. 1:18).

For the believer, there is nothing like the Word of God to exalt the name of God. We appreciate and reverence the Word only because it is the glorious means by which we come to know God and worship Him. Those who want to get to know God are constantly and ever in the Word of God. This is what gives us the basis and the impetus for glorifying God and worshiping Him in the congregation. Those who do not want to get to know God are not particularly drawn to sermons or to reading the Word each and every day. They rather find such activities boring, most probably because they are too self-focused to be bothered with the worship of God.

Verses 3-5

Now these verses testify to the deepest convictions in the heart of David, the psalmist. He speaks of how God has strengthened him through the darkest and most difficult days of his life. At the end of the day, true worshipers do not care so much about what people think about themselves, but what people think about God. So the kings of the earth persecute believers. What is of more concern is that these kings are not turning around and giving God glory for their accomplishments and blessings. The pride of man detracts from the glory of God, and this is an offense of cosmic proportions in the mind of the worshiper. Thus, the psalmist testifies that all the kings of the earth will praise God—even the wrath of men will praise Him (Ps. 76:10). Whether here or there, every knee will bow and every tongue will confess that Jesus Christ is Lord, to the glory of God the Father (Phil. 2:10,11). This is a consideration that renders great satisfaction to the heart of the worshiping believer.

From verse five it seems that these kings are voluntarily singing and praising God. This indicates a certain piety with political leaders around the world. And indeed, we have seen some of this, at least according to the testimonies of certain leaders like Patrick Henry,

Oliver Cromwell, King Alfred, Gustavus Adolphus, William the Silent, and John Quincy Adams.

Verses 6-8

How does one come into the presence of God? How is it that God gives grace to some and draws back from others? Why does the Publican go home justified in the parable, and the Pharisee does not (Luke 18:9-14)? The all important answer to these questions is contained in verse six. The Lord gives grace to the humble. After the powerful kings and their proud empires have disappeared into the rubble, who is left still standing but the meek and the lowly. Far above all the powers of the earth, God sits on His mighty sovereign throne ruling over all. Hence, we are far less concerned with the earthly kings than we are with the God of heaven (Prov. 29:26). It is tantamount that we humble ourselves in respect to Him. While He has some cognizance of the proud of the earth, He has no interest in any kind of intimate relationship with them. No proud person will ever be a friend of God. "He knows the proud afar off."

With confidence, the psalmist claims that God will deliver him from out of his troubles. He may feel very small in respect to the power of the enemy, and he may feel extremely small in respect to God. But, that's alright. God rescues the little guy, who cries out from his knees to Him for salvation. David is convinced that God will deliver him.

The last verse contains all of the encouragement anybody will ever need in this life. How many people are concerned that their lives may be wasted, or that death will put an end to all purpose for them, perhaps even land them in hell? Who can guarantee that all of their life's work will amount to anything in the long run? Of course, only God can assure that the work He has begun in us will be completed in the day of the Lord Jesus Christ (Phil. 1:6). Nobody but God can make a life worth living. If we were living in a chance universe, or if we were relying on ourselves or other people to make our lives worth living, it would never happen. Certainly everyone of us lives a flawed life—our work is flawed, our lives are flawed with sin and broken relationships. Only God can redeem these lives and turn something of eternal value out of them.

How do we apply this Psalm to our lives?

Are we concerned about our own lives ahead of the glory of God? Is our confidence and faith first in God, that He will perform the work He has set out to do? Almost everybody is concerned about seeking favor of man and the great leaders of the earth. However, every work shall be called into judgment. Since God is the ultimate Judge of the earth, it is our relationship with Him that matters most. Two questions remain therefore for every believer. Are we humble? And is God glorified? This is what matters above everything else.

When the wheels come off of our vehicle, we need to remember that God took them off, and He is going to make something better out of our lives. We must rely upon God to perfect the work of our lives.

How does this Psalm teach us to worship God?

There is only one way to worship God—with your whole heart. Half-hearted praise will never do. This whole-hearted praise will only come from a life devoted to God and souls that have been radically saved from the power of the Egyptians at the Red Sea.

Questions:

1. What two elements are crucial for our ability to relate to God?

2. Why is it no disrespect to praise God in front of presidents and governors?

3. What is the difference between the Publican and the Pharisee in the parable? Why did the Publican go home justified rather than the other?

4. How does God make life worth living?

5. What is the setting of this psalm, according to verse 7?

Family Discussion Questions:

1. What political leaders seem to have expressed genuine Christian faith in history? How might we be able to glorify God in the

presence of political leaders in our day?

2. How does the Word of God inspire us to worship? Give examples of how this has happened to you recently.

Psalm 139

Category: *Confession, Imprecatory*
Occasion: *Meditation on God's Presence*
Author: *David*

....

1 O Lord, thou hast searched me, and known me.

2 Thou knowest my downsitting and mine uprising, thou understandest my thought afar off.

3 Thou compassest my path and my lying down, and art acquainted with all my ways.

4 For there is not a word in my tongue, but, lo, O Lord, thou knowest it altogether.

5 Thou hast beset me behind and before, and laid thine hand upon me.

6 Such knowledge is too wonderful for me; it is high, I cannot attain unto it.

7 Whither shall I go from thy spirit? Or whither shall I flee from thy presence?

8 If I ascend up into heaven, thou art there: if I make my bed in hell, behold, thou art there.

9 If I take the wings of the morning, and dwell in the uttermost parts of the sea;

10 Even there shall thy hand lead me, and thy right hand shall hold me.

11 If I say, Surely the darkness shall cover me; even the night shall be light about me.

12 Yea, the darkness hideth not from thee; but the night shineth as

the day: the darkness and the light are both alike to thee.

13 For thou hast possessed my reins: thou hast covered me in my mother's womb.

14 I will praise thee; for I am fearfully and wonderfully made: marvelous are thy works; and that my soul knoweth right well.

15 My substance was not hid from thee, when I was made in secret, and curiously wrought in the lowest parts of the earth.

16 Thine eyes did see my substance, yet being unperfect; and in thy book all my members were written, which in continuance were fashioned, when as yet there was none of them.

17 How precious also are thy thoughts unto me, O God! How great is the sum of them!

18 If I should count them, they are more in number than the sand: when I awake, I am still with thee.

19 Surely thou wilt slay the wicked, O God: depart from me therefore, ye bloody men.

20 For they speak against thee wickedly, and thine enemies take thy name in vain.

21 Do not I hate them, O Lord, that hate thee? And am not I grieved with those that rise up against thee?

22 I hate them with perfect hatred: I count them mine enemies.

23 Search me, O God, and know my heart: try me, and know my thoughts:

24 And see if there be any wicked way in me, and lead me in the way everlasting.

The Point:

Meditating upon God's piercing knowledge of every aspect of our existence drives us to more trust, more confession, and more praise.

How do we feel in the recitation of this Psalm?

We are not lonely. To be known by somebody is the antithesis to loneliness. To be known very well by somebody we love and to be in the very intimate presence of that person gives our life a value that is outside of us. If that other person looks upon us with favor, then we will readily accept their scrutiny with gratitude because we know they know us well. This is how the Psalmist views his relationship with God. David feels God's right hand over him, under him, and around him. As we participate in this psalm, we feel the comfort and the security of knowing God's intimate interest in our lives.

The psalm ends with a call for the destruction of the wicked. To some this may appear as a vindictiveness that suddenly erupts within the psalmist. That cannot be the case here. Rather, we should see the intense love that David has for God and a deep appreciation of His hand in his life. We understand that love must have something of a jealous aspect to it. When we love something, we will desire an end to whatever thing is trying to destroy what we love. That is the nature of love. We cannot possibly approve of that which utterly despises God and His revelation. An intense love by necessity involves an intense hatred as well, especially in this sinful world where the hatred of God is so virulent.

What does this Psalm say?

Verses 1-6

First, this psalm consists of a meditation on the knowledge of God. What a difference between our comprehension and God's. Our knowledge is fleeting, imprecise, and shallow. God's knowledge is thorough, completely accurate, piercing, and utterly substantial and comprehensive. If this is the case, then God must know us better than we know ourselves.

God knows you through and through. There is comfort in knowing that somebody knows you. For example, the fact that a spouse or a mother knows you is a blessing because you are known by someone who loves you. This is one who wants the best for you, and in the case of our God, He knows exactly how to obtain the very best for you.

When Adam fell into sin, he broke relationship with God. He hid behind the trees in the garden, partly out of shame for his own sin and partly out of hatred for God. This is the picture of the natural man. He doesn't want to know that God knows him and everything that he does. When we come back into relationship with God through Jesus Christ, we gladly accept God's piercing eye and all-knowing heart, and we desire an amiable relationship with Him once again. Every day we wake up to the reality of God's presence, and we say with Jacob, "Surely the Lord is in this place and I knew it not!"

God's knowledge of us is intimate when we are living in covenant with Him through His Son. Unlike the wicked whom God knows afar off (Ps. 138:6), His knowledge of His own children involves a deep and vital concern, a connectedness to their every condition. A Christian father is always far more concerned about the goings-on in the lives of his own sons and daughters than he is with the neighbor's kids. He's attuned to their moods, their habits, their relationships, and their perspectives because he has bought into their development. How much more is God connected to His children?

The whole world pulsates with the life of God. Indeed, He sustains it all by the Word of His power, and He sent His Son to rescue this world from the curse of sin and death. His interest in this world, therefore, is vital, but His interest and knowledge of His own children could not possibly be more intensive than it is. "Such knowledge is too wonderful for me!"

Verses 7-12

Where shall I go from your presence? The prophet Jonah somehow thought he could escape the presence of God when he sailed the other direction, toward Tarshish (Jon. 1:3). God soundly corrected him for his ignorance and petulance. For most Christians, however, their urgent concern is whether God is present in their darkness. Will we find God in the valley of the shadow of death? When tossed away into a communist prison, will God's presence be felt? If there is anything we learn from the biographies of Richard Wurmbrand and others in similar situations, it is that God's presence is very real and thoroughly felt in the worst possible predicaments. There is always a "fourth man in the fire," when God's people must face the dragon's wrath. On the day that 31 men were delivered from a mine in Chile after they were encapsulated in what seemed like a tomb, half a mile underground, for 69 days, they left a carved message in the wall of the mine that read, "God was with us." Shift foreman Luis Urzua commented to the press, "The devil couldn't do anything because God was present." From the very depths of the earth, the men with faith testified in no uncertain terms that God was there. Many other men and women can also testify to the presence of God under the most excruciatingly difficult circumstances.

We are hampered by the darkness, but God is not. We are threatened by the devil, by tyrants, by despairing thoughts and stifling emotions, but God is not. His light overwhelms the darkness everywhere and nothing can possibly limit His knowledge and His love for His own.

Verses 13–16

Nobody knows the watch like the watchmaker. Nobody knows every board, every electrical outlet, and every pipe weld in a home like the contractor who built it. Similarly, nobody knows your personality, your mind, your weaknesses, your strengths, and your physical make up like the One who made you. There is no reason to believe that the Creator is any less intelligent or aware of His creation than the contractor and the watchmaker are of theirs. Certainly, the human frame and soul is far, far more involved than a house or a watch. This Creator doesn't throw something together haphazardly and then walk away from His creation.

Verse 14 needs to be on every page of every biology textbook produced. Today, we know 10,000 times more information about the human body than David would have known in 1000 BC. The human eye alone is made up of 2,000,000 moving parts and can detect up to 50,000 shades of gray. It can detect the smallest amounts of light down to a single photon and can work a dynamic range up to 10 billion photons. No camera or computer can focus on everything in its field of view as quickly and immediately as the human eye. Even the anti-Christian evolutionist Charles Darwin admitted the absurdity of his own theory of evolution when he studied the human eye. In his words, "To suppose that the eye, with all its inimitable contrivances for adjusting the focus to different distances, for admitting different amounts of light, and for the correction of spherical and chromatic aberration, could have been formed by natural selection, seems, I freely confess, absurd in the highest possible degree." (Emphasis my own.) Such contemplations press us to cry out with the psalmist, "I will praise thee; for I am fearfully and wonderfully made!"

Verses 15 and 16 underscore the careful planning and intentional purpose God brings into the creation of each person. He records "all of my members," which speaks of the DNA molecule, as well as all of the other cells, tissues, bones, and organs constituting the human frame. For every human on earth, he has written a code for three billion DNA bases that would fill up three gigabytes of computer memory. That amounts to as much information as would be contained in two-hundred 1,000-page New York City phone directories.

This passage shows the value in the creation of a child because God's hand covers the fetus in the womb (vs. 13). If this creative work of God is praiseworthy, if it is defined as marvelous and wonderful (vs. 14), then certainly there must be some tremendous value in the child who is still in his mother's womb. If the psalmist could speak of "my substance" while "I was made in secret," this appears as irrefutable proof that the unborn child has personality and personhood. That being the case, aborting a child in its mother's womb is the murder of a human person. This is the consensus view of 2,000 years of Christian theologians, pastors, and teachers who have studied Holy Scripture.

Verses 17-18

Now the Psalmist turns from God's presence and works into a meditation concerning God's thoughts. As he comes to realize that God is vitally concerned with every aspect of his life and has been since he was formed in his mother's womb, David expresses both awe and deep appreciation. God's knowledge is intensive and extensive. He knows everything about everything and everybody. This is the great starting point for all true belief. God's thoughts are higher than our thoughts, and God's revelation must never be questioned. Conversely, unbelief begins with the devil's question to Eve: "Yea, hath God said…?"

Verses 19-22

Now, the psalm takes what appears to be a strange turn. For eighteen verses, David has expressed His awe and appreciation for God's omnipresence and omniscience. But here he takes note of the fact that others do not reverence God in this light. This is not altogether unfamiliar to our world. In fact, almost everybody in our society today takes His name in vain. Most of the Western nations have done their utmost to offend God's law in the most egregious ways. They promote abortion by government funding, by trading baby body parts, and by murdering the child that God is forming in the womb of its mother. They aggressively set themselves against Christ's church and God's Word. Should a Christian pastor read certain "politically-incorrect" Bible verses in a public forum, he will be subjected to unmitigated scorn and persecution. This psalm is of great use when confronting the wickedness of a post-Christian, apostate age.

Therefore, David exclaims, "Surely, God will kill the wicked." Some will attempt to explain away such hard-edged language. However, we must be careful to uphold these truths. We know that God will slay the wicked either in hellfire or He will crucify the old man on the earth (Rom. 6:6, Col. 3:5). Either way, the wicked will die a most violent death. Did you think that the wicked would continue forever? We must not in any way lessen the impact of these words.

Nonetheless, the text gets even more difficult. We hear people tell us that we ought to hate the sin and love the sinner, but does that comport with these words here? "Do not I hate them, O Lord, who hate You?" We need to take all of Scripture into account when considering these words. Our Lord Jesus Christ impressed on us the importance of loving our enemies, and doing good to those who despitefully use us (Matt 5:44). There is a difference between God's enemies and our enemies. In a true sense, we do not know the names and addresses of those who hate God. We are usually fairly well aware of those who despitefully use us, because they have made some contact with us in their treatment of us. But how do we know which thief on the cross is in the process of repentance and looking to Christ for salvation? At any given moment, we have no idea who will bow the knee to Christ and who will not. Thus, the category of those who hate God must be general, and non-specific.

We say with the Apostle Paul, "If anyone does not love the Lord Jesus Christ let him be accursed" (1 Cor. 16:22). To completely reject the Son of God, the gift of salvation, is to declare oneself as an enemy (accursed) of the Father forever.. The hatred we have is a God-oriented jealousy, and it has nothing to do with personal vindictiveness towards somebody who killed our dog or drove their automobile through our backyard fence. There is a form of hatred that is a godly hatred. It must be a derivative of our love for God. It is a "perfect hatred," as described here in verse 22.

Verses 23-24

An undue focus on the material contained in the previous few verses will make us run the risk of giving in to Pharisaical pride (Luke 8:11) and judgementalism (Matt. 7:1-3). Therefore, the psalmist quickly balances out these bold declarations with a focus upon his own condition. The "wicked" are not the only ones who have to deal with wickedness. Believers must also deal with the wickedness that lurks in their minds and lives. We are anxious to kill the old man, along with the deeds of the flesh (Rom. 6:6, 8:13). To be anxious for the destruction of the wicked in the world without a primary interest in the slaughter of the old man and the deeds of the flesh in our own lives is gross hypocrisy. Indeed, the dead remnants of the old man are closer to us, and the noxious fumes of this dying flesh more distasteful to us, than anything or anybody else further removed from us. Of course, God will slay the wicked either in eternal hellfire (where the worm does not die and the fire is not quenched), or He will crucify the old man on the earth (Rom. 6:6, Col. 3:5).

This is the perfect spiritual conclusion to the eloquent words this psalm spoke earlier concerning the penetrating knowledge that God has of each of us. Given that God knows us so well, we need Him to search our hearts and reveal any wicked motive, purpose, and thought within us. We need Him to strip back the hypocrisies and deceptive perspectives that keep us from seeing the truth about ourselves. We shudder to think how easily we can deceive ourselves. Without the Holy Spirit clarifying the real me and the real you and convicting us of our sinful condition, there would be no hope for us. We look for divine conviction, and then we rely entirely upon Him for His salvation. "Lead me in the way everlasting."

How do we apply this Psalm to our lives?

- If God really does know everything about us, there is no sense in pretending that there is some secret thing about us that He doesn't see. There is absolutely no hiding anything from God. His eyes are in every place beholding the evil and the good. Fallen man wants to hide from God behind the trees in the garden. He will hide his sin until he can get enough support for that sin from others, and then he "comes out of the closet"—looking for public approval for his sin. True believers, however, won't allow themselves to do this. They will cry out to God, "Search me oh God; deal with me. Try me. See if there be any wicked way in me."

• Christians must defend the lives of children in the womb. Even in the case of an accidental death of a child in the womb, the Bible imposes a fine on the perpetrator (Exod. 21:22ff). The loss of life is treated as a crime. How much more egregious would it be if the child was purposefully dismembered and killed while still residing in his/her mother's womb? Moreover, certain chemicals used for birth control create hazardous conditions in the womb for the developing fetus by thinning the uterine wall. This is no way to treat a little person whose body is developing according to the purposes of the Maker.

How does this Psalm teach us to worship God?

Worship calls for a sensitivity to God's works and a careful observation of the many complexities and creative nuances built into His creation. We study the human hand or the human eye, and then we burst out in praise, "I am fearfully and wonderfully made!"

Worship declares open season on all that is wicked and evil. First, we confess our own sin and mortify our sinful flesh. However, we do not stop here. It is appropriate to declare God's judgment upon the wicked who do not repent as well. In this sense, worship is not confined to being "nice" and "positive" and "inclusive." Certainly, preachers must be bold and courageous to go after sin within and sin without, individual sin and corporate sin, open sin and hidden sin, big sins and little sins—calling for God's mercy and cleansing, repentance, and judgment—they must go after all of it.

Questions:

1. Why was Adam uncomfortable with God's presence after the fall?

2. What sorts of believers have testified to God's very close presence?

3. How does this psalm speak against abortion (the killing of a child in his/her mother's womb)? What other verses in the Bible speak against abortion?

4. What are two ways in which God will kill the wicked?

5. What are the differences between our enemies and God's enemies?

5. How do verses 23 and 24 help us to avoid the potential of falling into hypocrisy?

Family Discussion Questions:

1. Give several examples of how the human body is wonderfully and fearfully made.

2. Are we to "love the sinner and hate the sin?" How does that comport with Psalm 139?

Psalm 140

Category: *Deliverance, Imprecatory*
Occasion: *Spiritual Assaults*
Author: *David*

....

1 Deliver me, O Lord, from the evil man: preserve me from the violent man;

2 Which imagine mischiefs in their heart; continually are they gathered together for war.

3 They have sharpened their tongues like a serpent; adders' poison is under their lips. Selah.

4 Keep me, O Lord, from the hands of the wicked; preserve me from the violent man; who have purposed to overthrow my goings.

5 The proud have hid a snare for me, and cords; they have spread a net by the wayside; they have set gins for me. Selah.

6 I said unto the Lord, Thou art my God: hear the voice of my supplications, O Lord.

7 O God the Lord, the strength of my salvation, thou hast covered my head in the day of battle.

8 Grant not, O Lord, the desires of the wicked: further not his wicked device; lest they exalt themselves. Selah.

9 As for the head of those that compass me about, let the mischief of their own lips cover them.

10 Let burning coals fall upon them: let them be cast into the fire; into deep pits, that they rise not up again.

11 Let not an evil speaker be established in the earth: evil shall hunt the violent man to overthrow him.

¹² I know that the Lord will maintain the cause of the afflicted, and the right of the poor.

¹³ Surely the righteous shall give thanks unto thy name: the upright shall dwell in thy presence.

The Point:

While facing the most violent and insidious attacks possible, we must believe that the Lord will never abandon His own afflicted saints.

How do we feel in the recitation of this Psalm?

The Christian is regularly surrounded by forces that are more powerful than he is. Make no mistake—they are bent on his destruction. The man or woman of faith who realizes this will have mixed emotions. He is constantly tempted to be anxious or stressed. When we realize that our final state, our survival, and our salvation are always in the hand of God, then we return to thanksgiving. Gradually, as the psalm progresses, we gather strength and find the faith to pray with increasing confidence.

What does this Psalm say?

Verses 1–5

The situation is perilous; of this there is no doubt. The psalm breaks out with a cry for help. Whether these are physical threats or spiritual threats, it is hard to say. But the psalmist realizes that he is in trouble, and he is surrounded by enemies much larger than himself.

At this early stage in the psalm, the psalmist is on the defense and prays "defensively." He will shift towards taking the offensive in prayer later on in the psalm. For now, he prays that God would preserve his life from the violent man who is determined to destroy him.

We all live in this "present evil world." Therefore, we can count on malignant forces forming evil machinations against us. To ignore this fact is itself a danger to any who would live the Christian life. There is no way that, of ourselves, we could out-maneuver, outwit, or outlast the powerful forces lying in wait to deceive. For we know that "we wrestle not against flesh and blood, but against principalities and against powers, against the rulers of the darkness of this world." (Eph. 6:12,13). We cannot possibly understand the dark deceptions of the most insidious devils in the universe. We don't think like them, so how can we oppose them? Thankfully, our God is both omniscient and omnipotent. He knows the hearts of men, their purposes, their ill motives, and their twisted ways. He can and will thwart their plans. Of course, the wicked will never get the best of God or the church of the Lord Jesus Christ. Though this church may be infiltrated by the most duplicitous hypocrites, and though it be persecuted by the most vehement opponents, these enemies can never prevail against the King of kings and the Lord of the Church!

Though this world with devils filled should threaten to undo us,

We will not fear for God has willed His truth to triumph through us!

That which is wicked is best defined as "proud" (vs. 5). Where there is pride, envy, and strife, surely there will be "every evil work" (Jas. 3:13, 14). Therefore, it is not that difficult to identify where the wicked lurk and the snares they lay for the believer. Their pride will always yield slander or flattery, and every other evil work.

Verses 6-7

Now the psalmist claims a covenant relationship with God. Referring to God by His covenant name, Yahweh, David proclaims, "You are my God." This is the only basis upon which we may be sure that God will hear us and answer our prayers. If we are in covenant with His Son, Jesus Christ, we may refer to Him as Father, and He will treat us as His true children. This father-child relationship is assumed in Christ's Sermon on the Mount. "If you then, who are evil, know how to give good gifts to your children, how much more will your Father who is in heaven give good things to those who ask him!" (Matt. 7:11).

David also reviews the many times in the past in which God has been there for him, protecting him in the day of battle. He realizes God's salvation to be a powerful thing, as he refers to "the strength of Your salvation." He thinks of the Lord as covering his head like a helmet in battle. It is a helmet made of impenetrable elements that will protect the most vital parts of the human frame. After years in the battle, the warrior becomes familiar with this piece of armor and fully relies upon it to protect him. The spiritual battle is no different. We come to rely upon God as our chief defense.

Verses 8–11

This portion of the psalm gradually moves towards petitions that engage a more offensive battle. First, David prays that God would withhold any privilege or advantage from the wicked. All success in every endeavor is in the hand of a sovereign God. Should the wicked be successful in persecuting the righteous, it is only because God has given them that edge (as He did for Satan when the devil set out to persecute Job). The major concern, however, is not our protection. It is God's glory. When the wicked gains advantage over the righteous, and when they sense that they can blaspheme God with impunity, inevitably they will think they have supremacy over God Himself. They are emboldened and increasingly arrogant in their rebellion. Prime time television programs present Christ as a homosexual. Pastors who condemn these egregious sexual sins are treated as pariahs. God's name is taken in vain everywhere, and man glorifies himself in the media almost constantly. The psalmist's concern is that in their arrogance, they fail to give God the glory due His name. He insists that there must at some point be an end of their arrogance and a return to the glory of God.

Verses 9 and 10 bring out imprecations in even more aggressive tones. It appears that David is praying that his enemies be cast into hell fire. Does he wish this for men like Absalom, Doeg, and Saul? Certainly, we can apply such curses to the evil spirits that obviously infected Saul and others. In fact, our human opponents would never be so powerful were it not for the prince of the power of the air and the "spiritual forces in heavenly places." This is what empowers them, fortifies their towers of influence, and threatens believers with such spiritual, mental, and political force. Fundamentally, this is what we want God to destroy in hell fire forever...and He will (Matt. 25:41).

David does not want the wicked to gain a foothold. They seem to flourish for a little while, but their political position is always tenuous. They slip and fall quickly, as in the case of Haman, Ahab, Herod, England's King John I, and Germany's Adolf Hitler. The wicked promulgators of eugenics and genocide, like H.G. Wells, Margaret Sanger, Thomas Huxley, and others, are falling out of favor only a generation or two after their deaths. They were adored as progressives in their day, but not so much now. The same thing will happen with the tens of thousands of political and cultural leaders who have embraced sexual perversion, abortion, abortifacient birth control devices, feminism, Marxism, and other "liberal" ideas and immoral lifestyles. In a hundred years, history will look upon the entire Western world with its progressive, godless agenda as a complete disaster. Perhaps they will move on to a new set of lies. But, as for the old set of lies, they will burn into an ash heap of ignominy and shame. All the major news networks that mocked Christians, all the liberal university elites that led the modern apostasies, all the politically-correct print media sources, all the government-funded abortion promoters, and all the atheist legal attack groups will be gone. "Let not the evil speaker be established in the earth."

David speaks up with ever-increasing confidence, when he says, "Evil shall hunt down the violent man to overthrow him." One day there will be an end to the unmitigated violence against the unborn. A violent society that kills relationships and uses a hard-edged violent language in common parlance will not survive. The violent spirit that embraces sexual nihilism and vengeful blood-soaked films and games will come to an end. The cruel violence of terrorism displayed on the front page of the news almost every day will eventually come to an end. At some point, the earth will tire of it. More importantly, God will tire of it. And it is not unusual for the violent to meet a violent end at the hands of evil forces.

Verses 12-13

The psalm closes with a firm statement of faith. God's people cannot allow themselves to believe for a moment that these evil powers will succeed. As sure as there is a God in the heavens, He will come to the aid of the afflicted and the poor. They will be exempted from His judgment upon the earth. "Blessed are the poor in spirit, for theirs is the kingdom of heaven." God will maintain the cause of those persecuted for righteousness sake and those subject to false accusations and mockery from the mainstream media or academia. Jesus Christ tells us that the meek shall inherit the kingdom of God. May we all be found in their number!

The last verse offers the most comforting reminder of all. Throughout the years of our lives and into eternity, we will only find more reasons to thank God for His goodness, His mercy, and His salvation. There is no higher honor than to dwell in the presence of God .

How do we apply this Psalm to our lives?

Faith must lead us from a merely defensive posture to an offensive posture in spiritual warfare. We must believe that "greater is He that is in us, than He that is in the world." As long as we are in Christ, and His Spirit dwells in us, we can be sure that the enemy has no power over us. When we are under attack either spiritually or physically, we pray that God would defend us. But we want more than this. We want the destruction of all evil, an end of all wickedness and violence forever. So let us pray with faith that this would happen.

How does this Psalm teach us to worship God?

We are aware of the evil that men do, and the wickedness that sometimes prevails around us. As with this psalm, it is appropriate for us to mention these realities in our worship, but we don't leave it there. We pray for God's deliverance, but we don't leave it there. We end our prayer with a note of confidence that God will overcome all evil.

Questions:

1. What is the situation in which David finds himself while he writes this psalm? In what situation might we be inclined to pray this psalm?

2. How do we know that David understands himself to be in covenant relationship with God?

3. What are the enemies that Paul is referring to when he prepares us for battle in Ephesians 6?

4. Give several examples of wicked and violent leaders who flourished for a while but who God later cut down.

5. Why is the believer so concerned that the wicked be stopped in their violence and pride?

Family Discussion Questions:

1. Do we pray both defensively and offensively? Or do we err on one side or the other?

2. How do we view the attacks that come our way? Are we aware of the spiritual aspect, or are we merely focused on the physical elements?

PSALM 141

Category: *Deliverance*
Occasion: *Self-doubt*
Author: *David*

....

1 Lord, I cry unto thee: make haste unto me; give ear unto my voice, when I cry unto thee.

2 Let my prayer be set forth before thee as incense; and the lifting up of my hands as the evening sacrifice.

3 Set a watch, O Lord, before my mouth; keep the door of my lips.

4 Incline not my heart to any evil thing, to practice wicked works with men that work iniquity: and let me not eat of their dainties.

5 Let the righteous smite me; it shall be a kindness: and let him reprove me; it shall be an excellent oil, which shall not break my head: for yet my prayer also shall be in their calamities.

6 When their judges are overthrown in stony places, they shall hear my words; for they are sweet.

7 Our bones are scattered at the grave's mouth, as when one cutteth and cleaveth wood upon the earth.

8 But mine eyes are unto thee, O God the Lord: in thee is my trust; leave not my soul destitute.

9 Keep me from the snares which they have laid for me, and the gins of the workers of iniquity.

10 Let the wicked fall into their own nets, whilst that I withal escape.

The Point:

We are often afflicted by our own weaknesses, and while we are open to reproof from the righteous, only God can protect us from our own sinful tendencies and the attacks of the wicked.

How do we feel in the recitation of this Psalm?

Enemies lurk without and doubts within, and the pressures seem to increase upon the mind and soul. There are traps everywhere, and then there is our own tendency to sin and fall over ourselves. Verse seven captures a sense of weakness and complete brokenness. Our very bones are scattered at the mouth of the grave. Relief comes in verse eight, as once again we declare our utter dependence upon God to pull us through these trying and difficult days.

What does this Psalm say?

Verses 1-2

David cries out to God as a five-year-old child cries out to his father for help. Does this seem incongruous for a mighty man of war whose sword drips with the blood of the Philistines? First and foremost, David is concerned with his relationship with the Lord of the Universe. He sees himself in the right light. When our Lord said that we must become as little children if we would enter the kingdom of heaven, this is what He meant (Matt. 18:3). As children are completely dependent upon their parents, we must be similarly dependent upon God.

The great assumption is that God is favorable to His people, and we come before God as those who have been accepted by Him. We desire that God be pleased by our offering of prayer. We lift up our hands in prayer as a sign of dependence upon God, as a drowning man lifts up his hands for the deliverer who will pull him out of the deep waters. The burning incense on the altar in Old Testament worship signifies the prayers of the saints. We desire that the words of our mouths be found acceptable in God's sight. This can only happen when we come in faith through the mediation of Christ and by the inworking of the Spirit of God.

Verses 3-4

The psalmist is first concerned with himself—his own speech and behavior—in this song of petition. This concern is rooted in the fear of God, and a healthy apprehension of the weakness of his own flesh. While the believer does not fear death and damnation, his greatest fear is to offend His Lord. Sometimes Christians appear to be less self-assertive than those around them, because they take no confidence in the flesh. They may even be perceived as weak and timid. Nonetheless, true wisdom is rooted in the fear of God, and always includes something of a bridle for the lips. They will always be asking themselves the questions: Are these words necessary? Are they edifying? Are they truthful? Are they loving? The mouth has great potential to be either destructive or constructive, to bless or to curse. Therefore, the judicious use of tongue is one of the most accurate tests of a real work of grace in the heart of the believer.

The Lord's Prayer contains the petition "Lead us not into temptation." This is essentially what the psalmist is saying in verse four. It is usually ungodly company that will eventually lead astray the young man or young woman who departs from the heritage he or she received in their Christian home. Inordinate amounts of time spent with ungodly friends, ungodly Internet contacts, ungodly entertainment, and ungodly images (containing sexual content, wealth and materialism, or high fashion), will yield bad effects in the life of that young person. "Protect us from these things," we pray to the Lord.

When a believer watches a motion picture filled with cursing, revenge, adultery, fornication, wrath, strife, envy, and idolatry (much of which plays out with impunity), he can either partake of these dainties or leave them be. Should he do the right thing by critiquing it, arguing against it, and properly discerning its content, he will not be partaking in the portions that are dishonoring to God while he is enjoying the entertainment value of the product. If he ignores all of the problems with the content, then he partakes of its ungodly dainties comfortably and thereby corrupts himself. We pray this will not to happen to us.

Verses 5-6

The believer must always be acceptant of a well-placed rebuke or reproof coming from a man wiser and more righteous than he. Nonetheless, the chastisement he receives from his brothers in no way weakens his resolve to oppose wickedness and stand for righteousness. The righteous are both humble and bold as a lion (Prov. 28:1). The righteous are confident in God's truth, even as they realize the weakness of their own flesh. Thus, they must rely upon God's forgiveness and the righteousness of Christ, while they confidently speak the truth. They are humble and willing to admit their own hypocrisy because the standard of truth does not come from within them.

When the rulers are wicked and judges approve of wickedness, the message of the Gospel is often silenced. The righteous are mocked and sometimes imprisoned for calling the people to repentance and faith in Christ. However, when God brings these wicked forces down and silences the devil, the sweet words of the Gospel once again become more accessible to the masses. It is therefore the mercy of God that He puts an end to these wicked powers in the stony places.

Verses 7–10

Any Christian leader who is really in the battle will face continual oppression, overwhelming opposition, intimidating death threats, and unrelenting pressures within and without. As long as he is on this earth, he will hardly ever feel the persecutions let up. He will always be impressed by his weakness in the face of these impossible odds. Verse seven is hardly an exaggeration—"our bones are scattered at the mouth of the grave." This highlights the total inability of the man to carry out the battle on his own strength. Admitting one's brokenness or helplessness before God is the right position for the Christian. The meek, the broken in spirit, and those who cry out for mercy are the ones who inherit the earth and receive the kingdom of God. Our only hope is in God, and the only effective thing we can do is pray to God. We must not focus upon the enemy or the critic or even on our closest brothers. Our complete reliance is upon God.

Verses nine and ten do not speak of hypothetical traps, for these things are very real. Enemies of true righteousness are always out to snare the righteous. Our Lord Jesus Christ comes face to face with the worst of it in the Scribes and Pharisees. Indeed, those who follow Christ will face envy and malice among unbelievers and will be tempted to partake of their iniquities. He must respond with humility, truth, and love for his enemies. Here we pray that we not be ensnared by the temptations of the world, and thereby ruin our testimony and besmirch the Name of our Lord.

How do we apply this Psalm to our lives?

We ought to be sensitive to our own weaknesses, humble and ready to confess when our sin is made known to us. This is the proper frame of mind for the believer. As we mature, we become less trusting of ourselves and more trusting of God. So, when we receive a correction from a brother or sister, let us receive it with thoughtful graciousness. Perhaps the correction that comes from a brother or sister may not be warranted in every single case. However, there is always something to learn about ourselves. There is always more sin to be mortified in our mortal bodies, and we should be eager to address it. At the very least, let us listen when a brother, sister, mother, or father takes the time to bring us a correction.

The tongue is the best barometer of the heart. If you want to know the state of your heart, listen to the words you speak (or the words that you want to speak). We need God to enable us when it comes to guarding our lips and monitoring the thoughts and intents of the heart. This is an everyday spiritual battle.

How does this Psalm teach us to worship God?

Prayer is where worship best expresses itself, and the best way to approach God is in the spirit of this psalm—in brokenness. "The sacrifices of God are a broken spirit" (Ps. 51:17). We begin with affliction, mourning, and weeping (Jas. 4:9,10), and then God receives us.

Questions:

1. When we lift our hands in worship, what does it signify?

2. What are the four watchmen that need to be placed on the lips?

Whose help do we need to put a bridle on the mouth?

3. What should be the result of a well-placed correction?

4. How does verse seven describe our weakness and brokenness?

5. How does the world try to entrap Christians?

Family Discussion Questions:

1. What is the state of the tongue in our family? On a scale of one to ten, how much of a guard is placed upon our lips and hearts? In what ways do we need to address the sins of the tongue and the mind in our communications?

2. Are there any delicacies of the world that have corrupted our family? To what evil things might our hearts be inclined?

PSALM 142

Category: *Deliverance*
Occasion: *Abandoned, Isolated, and Persecuted*
Author: *David*

1 I cried unto the Lord with my voice; with my voice unto the Lord did I make my supplication.
2 I poured out my complaint before him; I shewed before him my trouble.
3 When my spirit was overwhelmed within me, then thou knewest my path. In the way wherein I walked have they privily laid a snare for me.
4 I looked on my right hand, and beheld, but there was no man that would know me: refuge failed me; no man cared for my soul.
5 I cried unto thee, O Lord: I said, Thou art my refuge and my portion in the land of the living.
6 Attend unto my cry; for I am brought very low: deliver me from my persecutors; for they are stronger than I.
7 Bring my soul out of prison, that I may praise thy name: the righteous shall compass me about; for thou shalt deal bountifully with me.

The Point:

Though I may be reduced to prison with no advocate on earth to help me, still I will hope that one day God will redeem me so I can sing His praises in the assembly of the saints.

How do we feel in the recitation of this Psalm?

There is no feeling as devastating as abandonment, especially when you are already facing harsh persecution and imprisonment. When the persecuted saint has been in the prison for so long that everybody, including his own wife and children, have forgotten about him, he will cry out these plaintive words to God. Here, the believer is brought very low, yet he still longs for the time when God will bring him out of the prison and enable him to lift up songs of praises once again in the assembly of the saints.

What does this Psalm say?

Verses 1-2

The first portion of this psalm contains four statements that more or less say the same thing. This repetition adds to the pitiful nature of the cry. It accentuates the desperation of David's condition. "I cried out, I made a supplication, I poured out my complaint, I showed him my troubles." This cry shows his helplessness and his urgent need for help. He also carefully delineates the specific problems he faces. Sometimes it is hard to put our troubles into words when we take our prayers to the Lord. There may be no easy way to summarize the various facets of the problem and the totality of the struggle. Nonetheless, we must do the best that we can. Although our heavenly Father knows what we need before we ask, it is still important that He hears from us. Calling on the name of the Lord and crying out to Him is how we are saved. It was after the birth of Enoch in the line of Seth that men began to "call on the Name of the Lord" (Gen. 4:26). It is no different in the New Testament era (Acts 2:21, Rom. 10:13). Those who do cry out to God and pour out their needs to Him are the ones who will be saved.

Verses 3-4

This second portion of the psalm describes the situation faced by the psalmist—not altogether unfamiliar to us. He is overwhelmed, perplexed, and somewhat paralyzed. His capacity to function physically, emotionally, and mentally has been seriously curtailed. Indeed, any Christian can be subjected to tremendous emotional and mental suffering. It is important that the believer realize that this suffering is not the totality of the renewed man within him. At the center of his being, there is still hope in God. This faith is more essential to his very being than the crushing emotional trauma that he is experiencing. David is content to know that God has ordained his path, every step along the way.

David has two problems. First, the bad guys are doing their utmost to destroy his reputation—or his life! They watch his every move, and critique him every opportunity they get. It's worse than that, however, because now David is abandoned by all his friends as well. He says that no man cares for his soul. Towards the end of his life, the Apostle Paul stood trial before Nero, a terrifyingly powerful, evil man. Paul wrote to Timothy, "No man stood with me" (2 Tim. 4:16). When the going gets really tough for godly leaders, they will more than likely be abandoned by all. Nobody wants to risk their reputation to stand by a man who is reproached by the whole world, especially when he is shamed by the most powerful men in the world. The devil and all of his powers are arrayed against him. These conditions are not unusual. The devil is always going after Christian leaders; there is no escaping the devastating attacks from within the church or outside of the church. Under such horrifying circumstances, the godly man is left with only one thing to do. He has no support on earth that can help him. His only hope is found in God.

Verses 5-7

This short psalm comes across as both powerful and poignant. It is one piercing cry for help. There is no need for wordiness. These last three verses contain the substance of the cry. As all other supports disappear and as all comforts and reasons to live fade away, this is what he has left. He confesses to God, "You are my refuge and my portion in the land of the living." He is not a depressed man. At this point, his confession smells of hope and satisfaction in God. Only God can save him now. So he lays out his predicament before the Lord in plain terms. The psalmist is oppressed, persecuted, and completely under the immediate control of forces stronger than he is. Since the 2000s, this describes something of the condition of almost every Christian leader in Western countries (as well as in many Eastern countries). There is very little political strength left anywhere in the world to defend Christians from persecution. It will only be by the supernatural work of God that Christians will be enabled to worship God freely in the years to come.

Freedom, for God's man, is not to be used for indulging in opiates and excessive pleasures. What God's man wants to do is to gather with the people of God on a daily basis and praise the Name of the true and living God—Father, Son, and Holy Spirit. Nothing delights his soul more than to meet in the company of the saints of God and offer sacrifices of thanksgiving. Obviously, this is difficult to do when he is cast into solitary confinement for weeks or months at a time.

The psalm ends with a certain confidence that God will deal bountifully with the persecuted soul. One day, the abandoned soul will find himself surrounded by God's people again. They will receive him, recognize God's grace on his life, and warm gratitude and praise comes in the assembly of God's people. What a great vision to cheer the soul of the man who is still in solitary confinement!

How do we apply this Psalm to our lives?

God will test each of us in different ways. When we wake up and realize that all of the supports we were used to relying upon are gone, how will we react? Some may give way to despair, but not us. It is in times like these that we turn to God in complete reliance and pray these sorts of prayers.

Do we always realize that God "knows our path?" When it appears that evil forces have gotten the best of us, are we still content in the realization that God "knows our path?" If He is attending to every sparrow that falls and if He has counted every hair on our head, then we can be sure that He is very familiar with the path we traverse (even when we walk through the valley of the shadow of death).

How does this Psalm teach us to worship God?

The believer is always looking forward to corporate worship, even when he is buried in the deepest dungeon and hasn't seen the light of day for ten years. When sitting in prison camps, ungodly men will only anticipate their next cheeseburger or mug of beer. Believers will instead look forward to the fellowship and public worship of the body of Christ. This is one reason why imprisoned Christians usually find themselves conducting prison ministries. They labor in the prisons to form their own churches. That is freedom enough for the believer when he finds himself in these conditions.

Questions:

1. What is the comfort David receives when his spirit is overwhelmed and his enemies are setting traps for him?

2. What is necessary for salvation according to Romans 10:13?

3. What are the two problems that David enumerates in this psalm?

4. How can it be said that David appears hopeful in this psalm?

5. Why does David want to be free from prison?

Family Discussion Questions:

1. Have you ever felt overwhelmed, as the psalmist describes himself here in this psalm? What kept you from complete confusion and despair?

2. When you are severely oppressed, what are the comforting thoughts that give you hope? Does the worship of God play an important part in your life's priorities?

PSALM 143

Category: *Deliverance*
Occasion: *Hard Persecution*
Author: *David*

....

1 Hear my prayer, O Lord, give ear to my supplications: in thy
   faithfulness answer me, and in thy righteousness.

2 And enter not into judgment with thy servant: for in thy sight
   shall no man living be justified.

3 For the enemy hath persecuted my soul; he hath smitten my life
   down to the ground; he hath made me to dwell in darkness, as
   those that have been long dead.

4 Therefore is my spirit overwhelmed within me; my heart within
   me is desolate.

5 I remember the days of old; I meditate on all thy works; I muse
   on the work of thy hands.

6 I stretch forth my hands unto thee: my soul thirsteth after thee,
   as a thirsty land. Selah.

7 Hear me speedily, O Lord: my spirit faileth: hide not thy face
   from me, lest I be like unto them that go down into the pit.

8 Cause me to hear thy lovingkindness in the morning; for in thee
   do I trust: cause me to know the way wherein I should walk; for
   I lift up my soul unto thee.

⁹ Deliver me, O Lord, from mine enemies: I flee unto thee to hide me.

¹⁰ Teach me to do thy will; for thou art my God: thy spirit is good; lead me into the land of uprightness.

¹¹ Quicken me, O Lord, for thy name's sake: for thy righteousness' sake bring my soul out of trouble.

¹² And of thy mercy cut off mine enemies, and destroy all them that afflict my soul: for I am thy servant.

The Point:

Persecuted, overwhelmed, and cast down into the darkest dungeon as it were, we still find encouragement in the memories of God's works, and in prayer.

How do we feel in the recitation of this Psalm?

This is a dark, dark, dark time in the life of the believer. It is during these difficult times that we say with the psalmist, "My spirit is overwhelmed. My heart is desolate. My spirit fails." It is utter helplessness. This persecution is well beyond the torment of body—the enemy is torturing the soul with demonic accusations, deep in the valley of the shadow of death. In these dark days, we come to realize in a fuller way that our only hope is in God. We respond by throwing ourselves entirely upon the mercy of God. Some comfort returns as we meditate upon the works of God and turn to Him completely, with a prayer for deliverance.

What does this Psalm say?

Verses 1-2

The opening words of this agonizing prayer may very well be the most important, for these words frame the relationship we have with God. It is important to know that David does not go to God on the basis of his own righteousness. We have no standing with God apart from His righteousness, which is shared with us by Jesus Christ. When the devil's accusations fly at us, we have to know our standing is only in the grace of God, by the imputed righteousness of Christ.

Guilt is such an omnipresent reality to every person born since the fall that people always think and act in terms of it. They may attempt to deny it, but blame, shame, and guilt is part of human life. Even our little children blame each other for this or that. The entire world is busy shifting blame. Whoever is best at shifting blame gets elected to be President of the United States and wins the popularity contest (at least for a short time). All economic and social problems are blamed on the previous administration.

The devil is an eager player in this game of guilt. He is called the "accuser of the brethren," and it is an apt title for him (Rev. 12:10). But we can say with the Apostle Paul, "Who shall lay anything to the charge of God's elect? It is God that justifies. Who is he that condemns? It is Christ that died" (Rom 8:33, 34). There is no condemnation to them that are in Christ Jesus (Rom. 8:1). That is why the psalmist is insistent that God does not enter into judgment with him. Man may accuse him with an egregious charge, but it matters not a bit as long as he stands justified in God's sight. For David, the doctrine of justification is not as carefully worked out as it is for the Apostle Paul in the book of Romans. Yet the doctrine is here in rustic form. No person can stand on his own merits in God's sight, for all have sinned and come short of the glory of God. Clearly, "By the deeds of the law shall no flesh be justified in his sight" (Rom. 3:20). Thus, David pleads with God that He would somehow, by His grace, forgo all judgment with him. This is our only hope as well, and we are thankful that God has found a way to make this happen. He has become both just and the justifier of him who believes in Jesus (Rom. 3:26).

Let us not underestimate the importance of this starting point in prayer. If God marked our iniquities, who could ever stand before Him? (Ps. 130:3). Nobody walking this earth has a clean record, and all are subject to accusations, human contempt, rejection, and various forms of retribution for their shortcomings. In the broad scheme of things, why do we care what men think about us? What really matters is our position as we stand in the presence of the Judge of the Universe, the God with whom we have to do. This is a billion times more important than any other concern in our lives.

Verses 3-4

These two verses describe the condition of the psalmist in stark terms. Bodily persecution is one thing, but soul persecution is quite another. Humans can torture the body, but God will at times permit the devil to torture the soul. This is equally or more agonizing to the believer than bodily pain. One does not have to be cast away in a communist prison in China to experience this dark night of the soul. The particular trial described here is long and drawn out. David likens it to the darkness of death. For a time, the believer is cast into confusion, perplexity, and depression. He cannot find his way out of the labyrinth the devil created for him. This does not mean he has lost all hope—not at all! He can still hope that one day he will find a way out of it, but for now he is caught in this labyrinth. It is a very miserable state of affairs. So much so, that the psalmist says he is overwhelmed and his heart is desolate. These are very dark days indeed for the child of God.

Verses 5-6

Under these intolerable conditions, it seems incredible that David finds any comfort at all. Though he may not be experiencing the power of God in his life at the present moment, there is this one thing that comforts him—and that is the record of God's wonderful works performed in the past. He never tires of telling of the great Red Sea deliverance, the destruction of the Midianites, and the victory over the giant Goliath in the Valley of Elah. Similarly, we would review again the victory of the cross of Jesus Christ, the great outpouring of the Spirit at Pentecost, and the conquest of the martyrs in the Coliseum. There are many stories to tell and retell, and they encourage our souls. We may not have received much comfort in our own situation, but we are thrilled to remember what God has done in the lives of others. The story of Christ's suffering, death, burial, and resurrection holds the most comfort for us, because we are following Him. If we are dead with Him, we shall also live with Him. If we have fellowship with Him in His sufferings (Rom. 8:17), then why wouldn't we also follow His path to resurrection? In the darkest dungeons, these contemplations give us immeasurable encouragement. It is the work of God in the past that gives us great hope for the future.

In these dire circumstances, there is only one thing left to do. Help is to be found nowhere else. Therefore, we lift our hands in the air and plead for help from God alone. Above all other things, we thirst after God. Nothing else will satisfy us in this world. Everything else is just more sand in this dry and thirsty land. Only God can water our poor souls with His presence, His truth, His peace, and His salvation.

Verses 7-11

The remainder of the psalm consists of several petitions that David lifts up to God. He starts off His prayer with a desperate tone—"Hurry and help me now, or never." Whenever our spirit is failing, it is because we need more of the nearness of God. Whenever darkness has settled over our souls, it is because of the lack of the presence of light. Whenever joy is lacking, it is because we need the Holy Spirit to remind us that we are the children of God (Rom. 5:2-5, 8:16).

Intellectually, we know that God is loving and merciful. At points, however, the believer may doubt God's love for him, or he just has a hard time seeing it. That is why the prayer of verse eight is that God would "make me to hear Your lovingkindness in the morning." Sometimes we just don't feel God's love toward us, and that makes us miserable. We know that we should feel it. Thankfully, it is only by the Holy Spirit of God that we can come to know this love in that deeply intimate way.

David confirms his trust in God in verse eight; however, in this present state of confusion he can't quite see the way to walk. He is completely dependent upon God to guide him through the minefield of temptation and trial.

Then, in verses nine and ten, he confesses a simple faith in God. From the outset, he cries out for salvation from his enemies, which must include his own sins as well as the great spiritual enemy of his soul. This is why Jesus Christ came. Every believer repeats this cry to God, with the confidence that the Lord has already provided this salvation. Once we have prayed for this deliverance, we ask that He would help us do His will. David submits to the Savior God as His servant. This is David's identity, and he will retain this identity for the rest of his life. He commits to following the Lord, as the Lord leads him in the paths of righteousness for His Name's sake.

Again, he prays for regeneration and new life (in verses eleven and twelve), as well as deliverance from the hand of the enemy. His concluding statement is a confirmation of his identity. "I am your servant." What better position to be in than to be the servant (and the son) of the all-powerful, all-caring, all-knowing, and ever-present God of the universe? Of course, God will deliver His servants from every enemy that afflicts their souls! Of course, the Lord Jesus Christ will be with us even to the end, as He promised (Matt. 28:18-20).

How do we apply this Psalm to our lives?

Sometimes Christians must go through what some have called the "dark night of the soul." In these darkest days of the Christian life, we should ruminate on every word contained in this psalm, and follow the thought process. We describe our situation in plain words to God, and then we meditate upon His mighty works. We recite the works of God from Old and New Testaments. Then, we recite the work of God throughout church history, and the work of God in our own lives in time past. Finally, we pray the prayer of verses six through twelve. We throw ourselves entirely upon the mercy of God, without reservation, without hesitation, and without half-hearted doubts.

How does this Psalm teach us to worship God?

We are a weak people, always. There is no strong pastor, bishop, elder, or teacher in the church who can claim strength outside of Christ. There are some who can raise their hands higher in recognition of their utter dependence upon God, but these are usually the leaders in the church. This, however, does not indicate an inherent strength in the man himself. It is only stronger faith in the Source of all strength. The one who is a "better" beggar for mercy is still a beggar for mercy. If we see each other and ourselves in this light, we will have a right estimation of ourselves in relation to others in the body of the church.

Questions:

1. How can God accept us, without entering into judgment with us?

2. What term is used to describe the devil in Revelation 12:10, and how often does he live up to his name?

3. What is the condition of the psalmist as he writes this psalm?

4. Where does David find his comfort (see verses 5 and 6)?

5. Why does David ask God to show him His loving kindness?

6. How does David identify himself in this psalm?

Family Discussion Questions:

1. How often do you feel accusations and condemnations from the devil? How do you respond to this?

2. What is the most comforting thing for you to think about when you are discouraged, cast down, or depressed?

PSALM 144

Category: *Faith*
Occasion: *Worldly Corruption*
Author: *David*

....

1 Blessed be the Lord my strength which teacheth my hands to war, and my fingers to fight:

2 My goodness, and my fortress; my high tower, and my deliverer; my shield, and He in whom I trust; who subdueth my people under me.

3 Lord, what is man, that thou takest knowledge of him! Or the son of man, that thou makest account of him!

4 Man is like to vanity: his days are as a shadow that passeth away.

5 Bow thy heavens, O Lord, and come down: touch the mountains, and they shall smoke.

6 Cast forth lightning, and scatter them: shoot out thine arrows, and destroy them.

7 Send thine hand from above; rid me, and deliver me out of great waters, from the hand of strange children;

8 Whose mouth speaketh vanity, and their right hand is a right hand of falsehood.

9 I will sing a new song unto thee, O God: upon a psaltery and an instrument of ten strings will I sing praises unto thee.

¹⁰ It is He that giveth salvation unto kings: who delivereth David His servant from the hurtful sword.

¹¹ Rid me, and deliver me from the hand of strange children, whose mouth speaketh vanity, and their right hand is a right hand of falsehood:

¹² That our sons may be as plants grown up in their youth; that our daughters may be as corner stones, polished after the similitude of a palace:

¹³ That our garners may be full, affording all manner of store: that our sheep may bring forth thousands and ten thousands in our streets:

¹⁴ That our oxen may be strong to labour; that there be no breaking in, nor going out; that there be no complaining in our streets.

¹⁵ Happy is that people, that is in such a case: yea, happy is that people, whose God is the Lord.

The Point:

We ask God for deliverance from the worldly powers that try to corrupt God's people, in hopes that we might see blessings, and spiritual and physical health, in our family and our community.

How do we feel in the recitation of this Psalm?

In faith, we grasp the tremendous contrast between God's almighty power and the weakness of men. While we are cognizant of the dangers and deceits of this world, we are far more impressed by the power of God. Then, we respond with gratefulness as we think of the blessings that come to families who are covenanted to God and are purged from the influences of the world. What a joy to see our children walking in the truth! What more blessed state can there be in this world than to witness generations of children and grandchildren faithfully serving the Lord?

What does this Psalm say?

Verses 1-2

This psalm brings together war and peace—the destruction of God's enemies and the protection of God's people—at the same time. These are not unusual themes, especially when we look at the history of redemption. At the Red Sea, there is both the destruction of God's enemies and the preservation of God's people. The same thing can be said for Noah's ark and the worldwide flood. These are pictures of God's redemption for the church.

This psalm introduces David as the great warrior whom God has taught to fight. Battle language is not unusual for God's men. Towards the end of his life, the Apostle Paul claimed that he had "fought a good fight." While it is true that God fights for us, He also teaches us to fight. We learn that our weaponry is not carnal (2 Cor. 10:4), and our enemy is not flesh and blood (Eph. 6:12). Between here and heaven, there is a battle to wage. Every Christian must face his Goliath in the Valley of Elah, and Apollyon in the Valley of the Humiliation. Our enemies are demonic powers, the rulers of the darkness of this world, and spiritual wickedness that dominates in powerful institutions of men.

We can only battle in the power of His might, in the strength that He gives us. If we attempt to take on these terrifying enemies in our own strength, we will most certainly be decimated. Any believer who has attempted it can testify to that. Although David is thankful for his ability to fight Israel's battles, his focus is on God's defense and intervention. Therefore, he refers to the Lord as his strength, fortress, high tower, shield, and deliverer.

Verses 3-4

When facing seemingly insurmountable enemies, it is good to contrast man with God. Whether it is yourself or powerful political enemies, it doesn't matter. Man is hardly worth talking about. "What is man that you would even take notice of him?" These contemplations bring everything into proper perspective. These thoughts humble us and comfort us at the same time. Man is so fragile; he is mortal and extremely vulnerable to disease, emotional and mental breakdown, and death. The most powerful man in the world has dementia within five years of retiring from public office, and it isn't long before he doesn't even know his own name. "His days are as a shadow that passes away."

Verses 5-11

Before reviewing the blessings of covenant community, we must go to war. In a temporal, physical sense, David goes to war against Israel's enemies in hopes that there will be peace and prosperity for God's people. However, it is clear that the psalm is speaking of spiritual conflict as well. The covenant community cannot exist if it is utterly controlled by the world, the flesh, and the devil. Many churches today have completely capitulated to the enemy so there is no war, no real casualties, and no suffering. However, a local church will never be truly part of Christ's bride if it is completely dominated by flesh, pride, lust, and worldly ideas and practices.

David calls for God's intervention in his battle. The enemy forces are defined in verses 7, 8, and 11. They are foreigners who are known for speaking vanity and falsehood. Instantly, all of us should recognize this to be the very definition of "the world." These false teachers were promoting anti-biblical ideologies and sinful patterns. In our day, they advocate the use of contraceptives with abortifacient capacities, and call it "choice." They promote self-centeredness in sexuality, marriage, church, and worship. Their message comes through loud and clear via media, advertising, and entertainment, although they would not admit that they have this agenda. They undermine the sovereignty of God and the fear of God when they teach man-centeredness in astronomy, biology, history, and literature classes. The Christian community often accepts these inputs uncritically. They don't realize these foreigners are speaking vanity and falsehoods, luring Christians into the idolatry of materialism by political agendas and speeches, glossy advertisements, storefront displays, educational systems, and success seminars. David reacts strongly against these powerful systems that specialize in marketing vanity and manufacturing lies. He rightly concludes that no mere human being can stand against the principalities and powers that rule over this ungodly age. The Christian church and the Christian family simply cannot survive where self-centeredness, self-aggrandizement, self-worship, and man-centeredness dominate.

Thankfully, the world's stranglehold was broken at the cross. As the Apostle Paul explains, it is through the cross that "the world is crucified unto me, and I unto the world" (Gal. 6:14). Our Lord Jesus Christ made a show of the principalities and powers in His cross (Col. 2:15). The prince of this world was cast out, and our Lord got Himself the victory there! Before Christ comes, we are under the control of the prince of the power of the air, the evil spirit that works in the children of disobedience (Eph. 2:2). We walk according to the course of this world and we are children of wrath, "even as others" (Eph. 2:3). Whereas David saw the enemy in the form of the dark and deceived nations that surrounded Israel, we have a clearer understanding of the real enemy because of these New Testament passages.

David sings a battle song of victory, praising God for His deliverance from these virulent enemies. There is a celebratory air in this psalm, as we come away with the true sense of our victory. "This is the victory that overcomes the world, even our faith."

Verses 12–15

The remainder of the psalm describes the blessing of the covenant community and the generational faithfulness that comes when the world's influence is quelled. Instead of rebellion, lust, deceit, covetousness, drunkenness, and strife, we find sons and daughters whose God is the Lord. Our sons bear fruit unto righteousness even in their youth. They do not feel the need to take four years to test out the world's party scene in drunkenness and debauchery at college. Our daughters are stable, solid, and beautiful stones from which come many faithful generations of believers. While this vision is a far cry from the pattern of generational rebellion that is so common today, we need to claim these promises and pray this vision to God. It is a test of our faith to pray like this. Every church needs to plead with God as David does in the first part of this psalm—that He would overcome the worldly influences that so easily corrupt our children and destroy our covenant communities in the present day. Every day, let us pray for children who are faithful to the covenant.

The blessings listed in verses 13 and 14 speak of spiritual blessings as well as material. If the church is distinct from the world, the divorce rate in the church will be much less than that which is seen in the world. The church's rate of illegitimate births will be a fraction of the world's. Of course, we will find in the church repentant sinners who have turned away from their former lifestyle. Those who aborted their children in the past now count children a blessing, and they may even adopt orphans. Those Christian nations populated with tens of thousands of biblical churches really have been blessed over the years. Organizations like the Heritage Foundation and Transparency International have identified the most prosperous nations, the freest nations, and the most honest nations in their annual surveys. Almost without exception, these are Christian nations or at least nations with strong Christian heritage. The vision contained in these verses (and in Deuteronomy 28) has been realized in recent history.

Individual families must be careful not to apply verses 13 and 14 directly to themselves. Some teachers in our day promote a health and wealth gospel—that each Christian must and will live in material prosperity. A more careful consideration of this passage cannot draw such a conclusion. References to "streets" point rather to a corporate blessing. Generally, God blesses entire communities and nations that are faithful to Him. Most of the Western nations today have huge debt-to-GDP ratios, unsalvageable birth implosions, and unsustainable economic and agricultural systems because they have rejected God. They have unleashed perverted and destructive forms of science in genetic engineering, created weapons of mass destruction, and conducted stem cell research using aborted fetuses because they do not fear God or worship Him. This new science has become exceedingly dangerous.

Nonetheless, the true people of God, the church should be a sharp contrast to the world, even in these days. In this set-apart covenant body we will find a people who are blessed with godly children and love for one another. These are the ones who have walked out of Sodom. By the grace of God, they have walked awy from its sexual nihilism of pornography addictions and homosexuality. They do not gorge on a materialistic lifestyle of debt and voluntary enslavement. The last verse provides the basis for these blessings. Blessed will be the nation, or the family, that rejects idolatry and embraces the true and living God as their God. "Happy is that people whose God is the Lord!"

How do we apply this Psalm to our lives?

"Come out from among them and be separate, says the Lord" (2 Cor. 6:17). Too many professing Christians love the world and hate their brother. They speak excitedly of the latest blockbuster movies produced by ungodly men where the Lord's name is blasphemed and fornication is committed with impunity. Then, they create division in the churches and refuse to bear all things, believe all things, and endure all things in love for the brother and sister. In this demonstration of their true affections, they prove themselves not to be followers of Christ. "Love not the world, neither the things that are in the world," says John. That means we pray against the world, we avoid all fellowship with the unfruitful works of darkness, and we do not touch the unclean thing.

Let us also desire children who are fruitful for the kingdom of God. We want to raise our children in the greenhouse of Christ, in the nurture and admonition of the Lord. First, we must have a vision or a desire for it. Then, we must pray fervently for God's blessings of sons and daughters who hunger and thirst after righteousness in their youth. Too many young people raised in Christian homes want to dally with the world. It is a supernatural act of the Holy Spirit of God whenever there is a child who remembers his Creator in the days of his youth.

How does this Psalm teach us to worship God?

Pastors and teachers in the church should preach and pray against the world's idolatries and ideas. This includes a wise understanding of what the "foods offered to idols" are in our society today. What are the cultural symbols that represent the ideas and idolatries of the day? To mindlessly accept every worldly idea, and every cultural practice and symbol will create a synthesis with the world. This will destroy the church, as we have seen many times over the last two hundred years. Though most of the nations around the world may be in rebellion against God now, the true church will always be a special place, blessed by God, and different from the world.

Questions:

1. How does this psalm speak of war and peace?

2. Who is David fighting against? What is the word he uses to describe them? What is it that we fight?

3. How did Christ break the stranglehold that the world had on us?

4. Provide several examples of how the world can infiltrate a local church and destroy it.

5. What are the blessings of the true people of God, who are protected from the influences of the world?

6. How do verses 13 and 14 not support the "health and wealth gospel?"

Family Discussion Questions:

1. Provide several examples of worldly ideas that are both vain and deceitful.

2. What are some specific prayer requests we can raise concerning our own family and our own church community? How could we pray for a more spiritually-vibrant church community? How can we pray for our children, in reference to the blessings iterated in verse 12?

Psalm 145

Category: *Praise*
Occasion: *Remembering the Goodness of God*
Author: *David*

....

1   I will extol thee, my God, O king; and I will bless thy name for ever and ever.

2   Every day will I bless thee; and I will praise thy name for ever and ever.

3   Great is the Lord, and greatly to be praised; and His greatness is unsearchable.

4   One generation shall praise thy works to another, and shall declare thy mighty acts.

5   I will speak of the glorious honour of thy majesty, and of thy wondrous works.

6   And men shall speak of the might of thy terrible acts: and I will declare thy greatness.

7   They shall abundantly utter the memory of thy great goodness, and shall sing of thy righteousness.

8   The Lord is gracious, and full of compassion; slow to anger, and of great mercy.

9   The Lord is good to all: and His tender mercies are over all His works.

¹⁰ All thy works shall praise thee, O Lord; and thy saints shall bless thee.

¹¹ They shall speak of the glory of thy kingdom, and talk of thy power;

¹² To make known to the sons of men His mighty acts, and the glorious majesty of His kingdom.

¹³ Thy kingdom is an everlasting kingdom, and thy dominion endureth throughout all generations.

¹⁴ The Lord upholdeth all that fall, and raiseth up all those that be bowed down.

¹⁵ The eyes of all wait upon thee; and thou givest them their meat in due season.

¹⁶ Thou openest thine hand, and satisfiest the desire of every living thing.

¹⁷ The Lord is righteous in all His ways, and holy in all His works.

¹⁸ The Lord is nigh unto all them that call upon Him, to all that call upon Him in truth.

¹⁹ He will fulfill the desire of them that fear Him: He also will hear their cry, and will save them.

²⁰ The Lord preserveth all them that love Him: but all the wicked will He destroy.

²¹ My mouth shall speak the praise of the Lord: and let all flesh bless His holy name for ever and ever.

The Point:

Yahweh God is great and good, both terrible in justice and incomparably magnanimous in His mercy, and He is worthy to be praised.

How do we feel in the recitation of this Psalm?

"I will bless your name forever and ever!" This is a personal song of praise and worship. Even when we are alone, we find great delight in lifting praises to God. We speak affirming words, grateful words, awe-inspired words, boastful words, concerning the Lord of our lives. In some sense men are made to boast. It is when we boast in ourselves that the words turn to sawdust in our mouths. Yet when we boast in God in worship, we discover great reward and excitement of heart that will increase in intensity. It is a life experience for which we will never regret.

What does this Psalm say?

Verses 1-6

There is no higher calling in life than to praise the name of the Lord our God! It is the highest purpose for which we were created. There is nothing more rewarding than to cast off the constraints of a self-centered, man-centered existence and shout the praises of God. Here the psalmist pours forth gems of praise, one after another, without any restraint. His heart is literally bursting with the grandest things he can think of in this psalm of praise.

Three words are used for praise in the first two verses. "Exalt" speaks of boasting and lifting up the Person and works of God. "Bless" is a softer term involving humble adoration (often expressed by kneeling). And "praise" is a joyful acknowledgement of an aspect of God's nature or work.

Primarily, the attributes that David chooses to praise in these six verses are God's kingly traits of majesty, might, and greatness. The psalm opens with the reference to "my God, O King," and it follows that these regal traits should be recognized. Our undignified and informal age usually fails to recognize dignity or majesty. The proud minds of small men can hardly recognize true greatness. If by God's grace we can see some of the awesome greatness of God, if we are struck by His incomparable majesty, we want to recite this psalm as His true subjects. Truly God is King over all of creation, and the Lord Jesus Christ is Lord over all. This praise includes a deep sense of subservience to the King. As one who is truly greater than we are, One who is majestic and great, His very nature and presence demands praise. He is "greatly to be praised."

In this section, David is lining up all the various sources from which praise will rise to God. He commits himself to God's worship forever and ever, which is a tacit confession of future resurrection and glory. In order that the glory of God would never wane on the earth, he commits the next generation to praising God's works also (vs. 4). Then, he speaks of other men, perhaps from other nations around the world, joining into this praise. God's praise must continue into eternity, with no gaps in between. Every day, the praise of God must resound from our lips.

Verses 7–9

These verses further describe our King in His goodness and graciousness. He is a beneficent King, who for thousands of years demonstrates kindness to those who live in rebellion to Him. His care for the earth is seen in the grocery stores, from which thousands are fed (most of whom live in rebellion against Him). Every drop of rain that waters the earth is an indication of the tender care of His creation. His compassion and graciousness is best understood in the real historical account of His Son's visit to earth. There He fed thousands who were hungry, on the mountain. He healed every sick person and every blind man who asked for healing. He resuscitated every dead person He encountered in His three-year ministry. This is our God with whom we have to do. He is gracious, and full of compassion; slow to anger and of great mercy.

Verses 10–13

The works of God also demonstrate His power and majesty. Everywhere, we see the fingerprints of God upon His creation. The godly man notes God's works in nature, in history, and in the world's events. He studies all of these things for one reason—to better know the works of God and to realize His praise. All of God's works of creation and providence shout His praise. Every nation that rises and every nation that falls, every animal born into the wild, and every field of grass is a testimony to God's praise. The entire world in the physical realm, indeed the whole universe, is one perpetual chorus of praise to the Creator. This is the way we must interpret the reality that appears around us. To bring any other interpretation to it is to embrace a lie and to deny the Creator the worship that is due Him. This universe is not the product of random chance. It is the deliberate, intentional, purposeful, creative work of Almighty God, and it must stimulate wonder and praise within us.

Therefore, the saints of God must talk of His power. It must control our conversations in and outside of the church. It must be our passion to share the mighty acts of God and the glorious majesty of His kingdom with the sons of men. Thousands of times, we have reminded each other that our Lord beat the devil at His cross. We glory in the historical acts of the church, since One stronger than the Strong Man robbed his house. Church history is a mandatory course for our children's education, because it is the story of the conquering Christ in history. We are ashamed that for too long Christians have taught World History and American History and Western History, but they have forgotten to tell the story of the glorious Kingdom of the Lord Jesus Christ. We remind each other that Christ is indeed head over all things to the church (Eph. 1:22). His kingdom is an everlasting kingdom, which has only grown steadily since AD 33. We delight to remind each other of all of the kingdoms of men that have collapsed, while the kingdom of Jesus Christ marches on from century to century.

Verses 14-21

The remainder of this praise psalm speaks of God's acts of providence and redemption. He feeds every living thing in due season. Only a very small percentage of the animals on this globe are domesticated: well under 1%. The rest of them are fed directly by the hand of God. Most of the species can easily reproduce themselves, because God sees to it that they do. Even the penguins in the brutal winters of Antarctica feed their young in the most unusual way. The males sit on the eggs for two long months, while the females fill up on squid, fish, and krill. Upon the return of the females, the starving males take their turn at eating while the females care for the young hatchlings. Indeed God does give these vulnerable, short-legged, flightless creatures "their food in due season!"

For us, however, He provides salvation from our sinful and miserable condition. Blessed are the poor in spirit, and the broken hearted, and those that mourn, because He raises them up and comforts them (vs. 14). David is careful to point out that the Lord is still righteous and holy when He draws near to those who cry out to Him. He cannot compromise His righteousness as He saves sinners from their sins (vs. 17). When we finally see the true state of our hearts, and sincerely cry out to Him for salvation, He will save us. "Whosoever shall call upon the Name of the Lord shall be saved" (Rom. 10:13). The soul that cries out as the blind man did when Jesus came near will most certainly find mercy. "He will hear their cry, and will save them" (vs. 19).

The psalm first assumes that those who cry out to Him really do fear Him. There is a healthy respect for God that yields a conviction of sin, a true sense of spiritual impoverishment, and a need for cleansing. The Lord also preserves them that love Him (vs. 20). While the reprobates and the wicked around us face the awful judgment of God, Jude tells us to just "keep yourself in the love of God" (Jude 1:21). Realize the love of God for you, and love Him in return. Remain in relationship. Abide in the vine.

Given all of these reasons to praise the Lord, the psalm closes with another warm sentiment of praise and blessing. If God is all of this, wise and good, powerful and majestic, then He is worthy of praise from the mouth of every person on earth forever and ever. Amen.

How do we apply this Psalm to our lives?

May our hearts be warmed by the memory of God's goodness. We forget a great deal, especially as we grow older, but let us be a grateful people that remember the many instances of God's goodness in our lives. Praise needs to be a daily part of our lives, whether in prayer or hymn. What a cold home it would be where there is no thanksgiving and prayer!

How does this Psalm teach us to worship God?

Our worship services should be full of the recounting of God's great acts of mercy and compassion. There should be abundant testimonies of the "memory of His great goodness" (vs. 7). All of us have stories to tell of how God saved our souls, how He saved our lives, how He provided for us in wondrous ways, and how He answered our prayers. We can tell of supernatural acts also, but equally important are the stories of His regular acts of providential care for us.

Questions:

1. What are the differences between the words "exalt," "praise," and "bless?"

2. How does the psalmist commit himself and others to praising God (in the first six verses)? What does he sign himself up for in these verses?

3. How do we see the goodness of God in His providence?

4. How does God's kingdom compare to the kingdoms of men?

5. Why is church history an important part of our children's education?

6. Why does the godly man want to study nature and history?

Family Discussion Questions:

1. Provide specific reasons for thanking the Lord, exalting the Lord, and blessing the Lord right now.

2. How much does praise make up the atmosphere of our home? What is the temperature of our praise? Rate it from 32 degrees to 212 degrees.

Psalm 146

Category: *Praise*
Occasion: *Political Elections*
Author: *Unknown*

....

1   Praise ye the Lord. Praise the Lord, O my soul.

2   While I live will I praise the Lord: I will sing praises unto my God while I have any being.

3   Put not your trust in princes, nor in the son of man, in whom there is no help.

4   His breath goeth forth, he returneth to his earth; in that very day his thoughts perish.

5   Happy is he that hath the God of Jacob for his help, whose hope is in the Lord his God:

6   Which made heaven, and earth, the sea, and all that therein is: which keepeth truth for ever:

7   Which executeth judgment for the oppressed: which giveth food to the hungry. The Lord looseth the prisoners:

8   The Lord openeth the eyes of the blind: the Lord raiseth them that are bowed down: the Lord loveth the righteous:

9   The Lord preserveth the strangers; he relieveth the fatherless and widow: but the way of the wicked He turneth upside down.

10 The Lord shall reign for ever, even thy God, O Zion, unto all generations. Praise ye the Lord.

The Point:

The Lord our God, rather than the state, is more worthy of our praise and our trust because He really can save the oppressed, the prisoner, the blind, the stranger, the fatherless, and the widow.

How do we feel in the recitation of this Psalm?

We come into this psalm with a sense of happiness and contentedness because we have seen the salvation of the Lord radically save ourselves, our children, and our friends. We think of what God has already done, and the potential of what He can and will do in the future, and we rejoice. We consider what God has done for us, and we praise our God with warmed and ready hearts.

What does this Psalm say?

Verses 1-2

The psalmist bursts out in a resounding call to others to praise God, and then he directs the same admonition to himself. "Praise the Lord, O my soul!" Theologians tell us that the great purpose of all of life is to glorify God, and here the psalmist actually lives this out. He writes new songs of praise. The worshiper seeks out daily venues for praise though he finds himself in a secularized church full of half-hearted praise. His heart is filled with reasons to praise. He utterly rejects man-centered religion that always stops short of unrestrained praise. Too many people today seek an experience and a feeling in worship. They seek to get something out of it for themselves. Rather, here the psalmist brings himself into worship and offers all of himself to God.

The praise commended in this psalm is perpetual. It is an every-day element of life in the family and church. As we get older, we begin to lose our physical health and strength. At points, we may have little mental capacity. Sleeplessness may curtail our ability to think or to emote. However, the psalmist commits all of the faculties still available to him to the task of praise. He may be reduced to the mental condition of a two-year-old as he falls into dementia. It doesn't matter. For the rest of his life, he dedicates his mind, his emotions, and his soul to the worship of God. As the sharks of death ravage his body at the end, he is still praising God with every cell that remains!

Verses 3-4

The remainder of the psalm identifies the basis for praise, by contrasting earthly powers with our Lord and God. State worship may be the major sin of all modern nations. Since the 19th century, almost every national government in the world has increased its power and promised womb-to-tomb security.

Millions of people have come to trust the state for their daily bread, their health care, and their social security. There was none of this in the 1620s, the 1720s, or the 1820s. Now, the democratically-elected politicians campaign on unrealistic promises. These liars promise to fix the health systems, and provide a better economy. They pretend as if they are in sovereign control over agriculture, plagues, viruses, economic forces, the character of the work force, the moral condition of men's hearts, etc. etc. These politicians lie to us. The media lies. The legislatures lie. The bureaucracies lie. The political parties lie. There is actually "no help" in princes, according to verse three. Is that statement an exaggeration? Not at all! Without God's intervention, these men are completely incapable of controlling the forces inside and outside their nations to deliver peace, prosperity, health, and salvation.

The euphoria over presidential candidates at their conventions cannot be matched by the praise for the true and living God in His churches. People scream themselves hoarse during political rallies. Their expectations for their favorite candidates are very high as they enter the elections.

Despite his brave promises, the politician will fail again and again. Every president will be a cruel disappointment. After awhile, even the electorate will become disillusioned. Since 1984, the approval rating for the Congress of the United States has fallen from 60% to 9%. Political leaders take the credit when the economy does well, and when it does badly they blame it on the previous administration. Even the most respected leaders plant the seeds of their own destruction. This includes George Washington, Abraham Lincoln, and Franklin D. Roosevelt. They are all but men, and their bodies have all rotted in the grave. They weren't even able to save themselves. How could they save a nation from eventual ruin?

Verses 5-9

In contrast with the masses that trust in governments, here is the righteous man who trusts in the God of Jacob. He is happy who finds hope in the Lord his God. Trusting in man is irrational for many reasons, but primarily because man is mortal, finite, and limited in what he can do. As some like to put it, "Even the president puts his pants on one leg at a time!" On the other hand, God has no limitations to His ability, His power and wisdom. He made the heavens and the earth, and His works prove His deity. There should be no question here. "All the gods of the heathen are idols, but the Lord made the heavens!" Man's great medical institutions are still very much limited in what they can do. They cannot raise the dead or restore sight to the blind. Much of modern medical technology is overrated. With all of his scientific development, man is incapable of increasing longevity by more than a few years. We have no interest in praising the false gods that man has constructed for himself. Rather, we want to serve the true and living God. For He alone is the Creator and sovereign overseer of heaven and earth. His truth is unfailing, and His wisdom is unlimited and impeccable. What is man in comparison to that? He is nothing!

Pay special attention to whom it is that God helps. It is the oppressed, the hungry, the prisoners, the bowed down, the strangers, and the widow that He reaches out to assist. He is especially concerned for those who are bruised and broken by the fall, humbled, destitute, and "on their last leg."

Physical weakness is not the main problem that afflicts man. He is severely hampered by spiritual blindness, by spiritual bondage, by spiritual starvation, and spiritual oppression. The devil has blinded his eyes, and holds him under his control (2 Cor. 4:4, Eph. 2:2, 3). The great deliverance needed can only come by God's mighty hand that sets the captives free and opens the eyes of the blind. Even in the worst-case scenarios, God can bring about the most phenomenal redemption with tremendous spiritual, emotional, and physical effects. Children who are kidnapped and enslaved under the most sordid and wretched circumstances in the slums of Bangkok have been wondrously redeemed, both spiritually and physically. These stories are truly wondrous, and the Christian church around the world is filled with men, women, and children who can share amazing testimonies of redemption!

Verse 10

Here is the great summary statement for the psalm, as the psalmist points out that our King in heaven will never be deposed. Indeed, the crown rights over the world have been granted to our Savior, the Lord Jesus Christ. Humans do have an innate desire to praise some leader or a presidential candidate. This is why they pour out their adoration at political rallies and parades. It is vain worship, and always disappointing. Our adoration and worship must rather be channeled towards the King of kings, and Lord of lords.

The end of the psalm is the same as the beginning. We turn to our brothers and sisters around us in the church, and we say, "EVERY-BODY, PRAISE THE LORD!"

How do we apply this Psalm to our lives?

Everywhere today, we find people trusting in the socialist state. This idolatry is the devastating sin of millions of people. Every true church must teach against the sin of state worship and call their people to repentance. The poor must refuse dependence upon the state. As we walk the path of repentance, our churches must return to privatized charity that relies upon God's provision, not the provision of the state.

How does this Psalm teach us to worship God?

When we come to church, we come to the assembly of God's people to offer sacrifices of praise to our God. We do not come primarily to attend a self-help seminar, or to hear what God will do for us, or to fellowship with the saints. We are come to praise. We come with sacrifices of praise and thanksgiving. May they be the best sacrifices our souls can bring.

Questions:

1. What are the faculties within us that we can dedicate to the worship of God?

2. What are the two objects of trust contrasted in this psalm? Who is it that most people want to trust today?

3. Typically, what are the things that politicians act as if they can control? Who is it that ultimately controls all of these things?

4. Why is God a good object of our trust, according to this psalm?

5. Who are the people that God is most ready to help?

6. How is God described in the last verse of the psalm, and how does this remind us of His Son Jesus Christ?

Family Discussion Questions:

1. What is our family's view of government welfare programs? How do we live in such a way that we clearly do not trust in the state?

2. Do we have stories to tell, right now, of God's great deliverance from Satan's bondage and blindness?

PSALM 147

Category: *Praise*
Occasion: *Viewing Nature*
Author: *Unknown*

....

1 Praise ye the Lord: for it is good to sing praises unto our God; for it is pleasant; and praise is comely.

2 The Lord doth build up Jerusalem: he gathereth together the outcasts of Israel.

3 He healeth the broken in heart, and bindeth up their wounds.

4 He telleth the number of the stars; he calleth them all by their names.

5 Great is our Lord, and of great power: his understanding is infinite.

6 The Lord lifteth up the meek: he casteth the wicked down to the ground.

7 Sing unto the Lord with thanksgiving; sing praise upon the harp unto our God:

8 Who covereth the heaven with clouds, who prepareth rain for the earth, who maketh grass to grow upon the mountains.

9 He giveth to the beast his food, and to the young ravens which cry.

10 He delighteth not in the strength of the horse: he taketh not pleasure in the legs of a man.

11 The Lord taketh pleasure in them that fear him, in those that hope in his mercy.

12 Praise the Lord, O Jerusalem; praise thy God, O Zion.

13 For He hath strengthened the bars of thy gates; he hath blessed thy children within thee.

14 He maketh peace in thy borders, and filleth thee with the finest of the wheat.

15 He sendeth forth his commandment upon earth: his word runneth very swiftly.

16 He giveth snow like wool: he scattereth the hoarfrost like ashes.

17 He casteth forth his ice like morsels: who can stand before his cold?

18 He sendeth out his word, and melteth them: he causeth his wind to blow, and the waters flow.

19 He sheweth his word unto Jacob, his statutes and his judgments unto Israel.

20 He hath not dealt so with any nation: and as for his judgments, they have not known them. Praise ye the Lord.

The Point:

While we stand outside and take in the awesome view of the stars, the clouds, the fields, and the snow on the mountains, we consider God's goodness to His people.

How do we feel in the recitation of this Psalm?

We are thrilled at the view of God's awesome creation. We are even more awestruck as we can make out His fingerprints on the stars, the clouds, and the snow in the mountains. Then we are even more moved by the sense of God's hand upon us, His special care for us, His people. Finally, we come to realize that the beauty of God's praise transcends the beauty of the creation itself!

What does this Psalm say?

Verse 1

There are many good things to do in life, but praising God is man's highest good. There is nothing more rewarding, more delightful, more beautiful, and more noble than to commend the Lord of the universe and to appreciate His works. Humans are more ennobled when they appreciate that which is beautiful and noble in art and culture. The appreciation of good music created by gifted men and women lends a certain depth and richness to their lives. We are most inspired, uplifted, and ennobled, however, when we consider the ultimate Creator in His personality, His nature, and His works. What is the value of all the award ceremonies for beauty, sports, and entertainment, in which humans are always rewarding each other? Such celebrations become empty and degrading when God is taken out of the picture.

Modern worship is expected to render a certain feeling or experience to the worshiper. Man worships for his own sake, and he is still at the center. However, the best worship discovers something about God and returns sincere and heart-deep praise to Him. The true worshiper finds great satisfaction and enjoyment, not in a superficial, emotional way, but in the sense that he has plumbed the depths of life's purpose. May God help us to distinguish between empty, man-centered worship and true worship in this day of apostasy.

Praise and song are also intimately related in this first verse. In Christian worship, you cannot have one without the other. Singing is a daily routine among those whose hearts are filled with thanksgiving and awe for the Lord God.

Verses 2-7

Throughout this psalm, we look at God's works in nature and then God's work and interest in us. We learn something about God in viewing His creation, and then we realize that this is the God that relates to us, His people. This connection is made at least four times in the psalm.

It is appropriate to begin with the most blessed work of God—that of His work in His people. The Lord Jesus said He would build His church, and the gates of hell would not prevail against it (Matt. 16:18). At the end of the whole world, the people of God will gather to praise the name of Jesus who has redeemed them "out of every kindred, and tongue, and people, and nation" (Rev. 5:9,10; 19:7). He has found the outcasts of Israel and among the other nations and He has gathered them into a new people identified by the Name of His Son. Glorious work indeed! Creation is magnificent, but the redemption He brings to the miserable, the lost, the blind, and the hell-bound sinners is more impressive. His ministry of redemption comes to those whose hearts have been broken by a sense of their own sinfulness and lost condition (Ps. 51:1-17). Those who are bruised and broken, mangled in spirit, and sensitive to their own condition are the ones He helps. Here we see the tenderness of our Savior God and His vital interest in some poor, isolated soul. He reaches out to them and gathers them into His family.

If for a moment someone might think he could be lost from God's view on this third rock from the sun, the psalmist quickly follows with verse four. God calls every star by its own name. None of these quadrillions upon quadrillions of stars are lost to the Lord's attention. After all, this is His world. He made every part of it, and He knows everything about it. These contemplations bring us back to realize God's absolute power and infinite knowledge and understanding (vs. 5). Man's greatest creations are minuscule when set next to Mount Everest. Michelangelo's murals are not nearly so gorgeous or large as a sunset over the mountains. Man's total knowledge of the atom is only a tiny fraction of God's knowledge of it. Man's knowledge includes all of the hundreds of thousands of pages of textbooks and mathematical calculations attempting some rough approximation of God's blueprints. But there is no limit to God's power. It doesn't take Him more effort to make six billion stars than it does for Him to create a single atom. He is not worn out or intimidated by the problems of the universe.

In human society, we seldom see powerful people hanging around the poor and the downtrodden. The rich are almost always attending fancy dinners and talking about how they will make more money and gain more power and influence. Our God, however, isn't really all that interested in the rich and the powerful. He spends most of His time with fishermen and publicans. He more or less ignores the rich, except when one asks Him to heal His son (John 4:49ff). Our all-powerful God is most interested in helping the most humble sinners. The Most Powerful draws near to the most humble. This is one of the most fundamental principles of the Christian faith—and perhaps the most fundamental to the doctrine of our salvation. Meanwhile, the proud and wicked man doesn't stand a chance against the all-powerful God of the universe (vs. 6b).

Thus far, we have a twofold reason to praise the Lord. He is great, powerful, and wise, but He also takes a special interest in the humble. This is an awe-inspiring meditation. Let us sing unto the Lord with thanksgiving!

Verses 8-11

In these verses, we again stand in the outdoors and we behold God's natural creation. Do you ever grow tired of looking at the heavens, the clouds, the fields, and the mountains? The mighty cloud formations just above your head carry tons of water to moisturize the plants growing over millions of acres. How many blades of grass grow on that hill over there? Each plant is cared for by the hand of our heavenly Father, that He might provide food for the animals and for man. Meteorologists estimate that hurricane clouds will carry as much as 240 million tons of water—the weight of 2400 aircraft carriers. This demonstrates something of the power of God, and the wisdom and care He puts into watering the earth.

Verse ten turns back to God's dealings with men. Again we are reminded that the Creator of heaven and earth is not impressed by the strength of human armies and powerful governments. Men are enamored by the power of the state and its formidable military strength. Even among Christians, there is a a undue emphasis on "making an impact" as measured by "bodies, bucks, and buildings." But what delights our God is a man who fears Him and hopes in His mercy. Here is another distilled description of the faith. It is the man who trembles in the presence of God, but in his trembling he lifts his arms to the heavens. There he stands for hours upon hours, and days upon days, with his arms in the air waiting for God's mercy. He waits and hopes. He never gives up on hoping in the mercy of God.

The Lord our God takes great delight in the man who waits upon His mercy. That father and mother who finds a deep spiritual void in their children come to God in prayer. They depend upon the mercy of God, and they pray in hope for years upon years. They have no idea how or when the Lord will answer their prayers. But they pray, believing and hoping in a merciful God. Based on all that we know about God's power, wisdom, and mercy, we live with an outrageously hopeful outlook. The current conditions may seem to present a lost cause, but our eyes are focused on the heavens and we are hoping in the mercy of God. This is what God likes.

Verses 12-20

Now, the psalm turns to the people of God who are gathered and points out the blessing of the body of Christ. The Apostles, also, love to offer prayers of thanksgiving over the churches in their epistles (Eph. 1:16, 1 Thess. 1:2, 3 John 2-4). When we gather on Sundays, we ought to thank the Lord for the body of saints sitting about us. It is the most glorious accomplishment of our Redeemer God. He has loaded us with physical blessings, yes, but also every spiritual blessing in the heavenly places (Eph. 1:3). Granted, there are some assemblies in the throes of apostasy in which divisions, schisms, and conflicts dominate. There is no peace for the wicked, and the Gospel of Christ seems to have no real impact upon these folks. Within the true fellowship of believers, however, He is our peace. He breaks down the middle wall of partition where there were two-thousand-year conflicts that separated man and man (Eph. 2:14). The true church will find peace within and between brothers and sisters in Christ. There will be peacemaking, restoration, reconciliation, and forgiveness. These are reasons to gather for praise and worship in the church!

Once again, we return to God's providential hand over nature in verse 15. The psalmist points out that God's Word takes command over nature, and then he compares it to God's powerful Word used in discipling the nations in verses 19 and 20.

The winter storms come as the deliberate, authoritative will of God communicated by His word. He speaks and the snow falls, and the frost decorates the billions of pine needles in the forests on the mountains. Imagine how much work it would take for a painter to paint each of the pine needles in order to create such a gorgeous magical scene! When the time is right, He sends His Word again (vs. 18) and the snow on the mountains melts. The waters rush into roaring rivers and water the plains, the fields, and the villages all the way to the sea.

Who can stand before His cold? Snow presents a dangerous and hard-edged beauty. It is usually best enjoyed from inside the lodge, unless we are dressed well for it. Through the years, many have died in snowstorms, or have frozen to death in the cold. We are reminded of the power, the beauty, and the dangerous judgment of God in His works.

As sure as the Word of God spreads the snow and waters over millions of acres of land throughout the world, His Word flows throughout the world. He sends His Word out, and it does not return to Him void.

"For as the rain cometh down, and the snow from heaven, and returneth not thither, but watereth the earth, and maketh it bring forth and bud, that it may give seed to the sower, and bread to the eater: so shall my word be that goeth forth out of my mouth: it shall not return unto me void, but it shall accomplish that which I please, and it shall prosper in the thing whereto I sent it" (Isa. 55:10, 11).

Through the patient work of evangelists, pastors, and teachers, the nations are discipled through the centuries. Every tribe and nation are receiving the commandments, statutes, and judgments of the God of Israel. Nations that did not know the judgments of God have come to know them. In 843 AD, King Rastislav from Bohemia requested missionaries to come teach the people to "observe Christian law." Two brothers, Methodius and Cyril came and developed a written language. They translated the New Testament into the Bohemian language right away, and provided Rastislav with the first civil law code. This is only one example of how nations have been discipled over the two thousand years of kingdom work that has passed. Throughout the last three thousand years, the Lord has blessed certain nations with a godly heritage while leaving other nations alone. He is sovereign over individuals and nations, and takes His Word where He deigns to take it. Praise ye the Lord!

How do we apply this Psalm to our lives?

Hearts that are filled with the urge to praise will break out spontaneously in worship with song. The *Doxology*, the *Gloria Patri*, and the praise psalms will be part of the routine of any Christian family. Children raised in a Christian home will hear hymns of thanksgiving from their godly fathers and mothers on a regular basis. These Christian homes are few and far between these days, but you will recognize them immediately by their praise in song.

When a proud and wealthy people forget to worship and thank God for their blessings, they will always sink into decadence. The seeds of this rebellion are always seen when families skip worship for sports games, wealth, entertainment, and vacations. Their hearts are manifest in their priorities.

How does this Psalm teach us to worship God?

We must draw all of God's works into consideration when we worship. What we can see with our eyes (in nature) can be helpful to better understand how He works in our salvation. We can learn of His power and mercy. Thus, it is appropriate that the worship begin with the recognition of His physical blessings and His tremendous work in the physical world. We must, however, not leave it there. We must move on to more spiritual blessings and spiritual application.

Questions:

1. What is the connection that is made four times throughout this psalm?

2. How is it comforting to know that God has named every one of the stars?

3. What teaching is fundamental to our salvation (our soteriology)?

4. With whom is God not so impressed? Where does He find delight?

5. What is unique about snow?

6. How does Isaiah 55 tie into this passage?

Family Discussion Questions:

1. Is worship the most fulfilling and ennobling part of our lives? What effect does worship have upon us?

2. Are you hoping in God's mercy? For what things are you waiting upon God (in terms of your own life and the lives of others)?

PSALM 148

Category: *Praise*
Occasion: *Age-integrated Worship*
Author: *Unknown*

· ·

1   Praise ye the Lord. Praise ye the Lord from the heavens: praise him in the heights.
2   Praise ye him, all his angels: praise ye him, all his hosts.
3   Praise ye him, sun and moon: praise him, all ye stars of light.
4   Praise him, ye heavens of heavens, and ye waters that be above the heavens.
5   Let them praise the name of the Lord: for he commanded, and they were created.
6   He hath also stablished them for ever and ever: he hath made a decree which shall not pass.
7   Praise the Lord from the earth, ye dragons, and all deeps:

⁸ Fire, and hail; snow, and vapours; stormy wind fulfilling his word:

⁹ Mountains, and all hills; fruitful trees, and all cedars:

¹⁰ Beasts, and all cattle; creeping things, and flying fowl:

¹¹ Kings of the earth, and all people; princes, and all judges of the earth:

¹² Both young men, and maidens; old men, and children:

¹³ Let them praise the name of the Lord: for his name alone is excellent; his glory is above the earth and heaven.

¹⁴ He also exalteth the horn of his people, the praise of all his saints; even of the children of Israel, a people near unto him. Praise ye the Lord.

The Point:

We call on everything around us to praise the Lord, for He is glorious above all and He makes the praise of our lips glorious.

How do we feel in the recitation of this Psalm?

The entire book of Psalms seems to be working towards a crescendo as we approach the end. The sentiment is exaltation at the highest level that is capable of being expressed by humans. We are in awe of God's works. With each successive verse, the volume increases, the tone becomes more insistent, and the thrill to the soul more intense. As we come to see more clearly that our God is worthy to be praised, we throw our hearts, our voices, our minds, and our souls into His praise with all the energy that is within us.

What does this Psalm say?

Verses 1-6

As we approach the psalm, we must picture ourselves standing in the middle of the world where we can see all of God's creation surrounding us. We stand and preach, as it were, to the whole universe about us. We admonish and exhort, encourage and coach, all of the voices to resonate the same message of praise. We fill the position of the choir director for the entire world. In this role, we are insistent, commanding, fervent, intense, and unrelenting.

The first section of the choir is not the bass or the tenor; it is the heavens and all that is above the earth. We begin with the angels, the very highest of God's created order. The angels are created for this purpose, so of course they will be more than wiling to cooperate in this great chorus of praise. This is the function of the seraphim in Isaiah's vision (Isa. 6:1-6). The angels fall on their faces and worship God, as we read in Revelation 7:11. Day and night without ceasing, the living creatures cry out "Holy, holy, holy, Lord God Almighty, which was, and is, and is to come." No creature, regardless of its state or power, is exempted from this holy duty.

After the angels, we command the sun and moon and stars to praise God. The waters in the clouds are commanded likewise to praise our covenant God! When we praise the name of the Lord, we praise Him for His reputation. His works establish His reputation. This is the case with all of us; as a great architect is known by his works, our God is known by His magnificent creation. When we praise human creators, we are especially impressed that their genius came about through many hours of work. It was the assiduous persistence of the Wright brothers who applied themselves for thousands of hours to the research and development of flight that warrant the recognition of men. With our God, however, His creation came into existence by His mere command. This is far more impressive to us than the works of men. "He commanded, and they were created."

The works of men rust away in the junkyards after forty or fifty years. But God's works continue for millennia. His stars could warm the planets for billions of years before burning out. Our sun does not shine and our earth does not rotate by random chance. The regularity of life is ordained by God, and His decree is absolutely certain until the end of the world.

Verses 7-10

After we direct the choirs of the universe, our attention is drawn to the surface of the earth. We call all of creation, from the depths of the Mariana Trench to the heights of Mount Everest, to this praise. Well up into the time of Abraham, dragons and great dinosaurs were likely living for centuries and growing to very large sizes. Tales of these great sea creatures and land creatures were told in many cultures in the earth. Still to this day, the great whales and sharks that roam the seas manifest the glory of God their Creator. More recently, scientists have discovered other mysterious creatures, very ugly and bizarre-looking sea animals roaming the depths of the Mariana Trench. All of these manifest the glory of their Creator.

Next, we call the elements of fire, hail, snow, and storms to the task of praise. These are powerful forces that can upset entire cities and states for weeks, months, and sometimes years. Man's technology cannot stand against these storms; it can only mop up the disaster areas after the fact. Only a fool would refuse to respond in fear and reverence for God when he encounters these violent storms.

Then, we move on to call the mountains, the hills, the fruit-bearing trees, and the mighty pines, cedars, and oak trees to praise Him. Again, the largest earth-moving equipment produced by man is minuscule in comparison with the mightiest mountain the world. It would take 22 billion loads to remove Everest using the world's largest bulldozer, the Komatsu 575A, capable of removing 2430 cubic feet of material at a time. The earth's fruit trees and the wood-bearing trees produce food, shelter, and energy for six billion people around the globe. These mighty, beautiful trees that grow up out of a tiny seed or acorn strike us as magical, supernatural creation. One seed that yields a beautiful tree providing bushels and bushels of fruit over thirty years, is just as impressive as the feeding of the five thousand in three hours on the hillside east of Galilee.

We call the land animals, the bugs, and the birds to lend their voices to this chorus of praise (vs. 10). Everything that bears the mystery of life—the chains of proteins informed by the genius of DNA, producing movement and capable of reproduction—is a testimony to the Source of all life and the genius of life. Praise ye the Lord!

Verses 11-14

Finally, we arrive at us. We think about the most powerful men who rule and judge in the earth. We call them to praise the Lord. To refuse to give God the glory is a cosmic treachery of the highest sort. When the Supreme Court of the United States rejected prayer and worship in the public schools, they sealed the fate of the nation. Their pride was further manifested in their advocacy of mass destruction of human life (in 1973) and the destruction of God's ordinance of marriage (in 2015). The glorification of man at the very highest levels usurps God's glory. At any point, however, these powerful men and women may repent and join into the praise of the universe to the God who is worthy of all praise.

Finally, we look around the church building where human beings are gathered, and we call every voice to join in unison in praise and worship. We fully expect old men, young men, maidens, and children to participate in the worship. God calls the church together, young and old, to signify a cross-generational worship.

Psalm 145:4 becomes a reality in our services! "One generation shall praise thy works to another, and shall declare thy mighty acts."

We will not contaminate this praise with accolades for anybody else. There will be no standing ovation for the preacher or the musician. When it comes to God's glory, He is in a category by Himself. His name alone is excellent in all the earth.

Yet, He chooses to raise up His people and to honor His church (vs. 14). Though our praise may be flawed, He turns it into something glorious. Though He is transcendent in His glory, we are reminded in the very last words of this psalm that He is also very near to us. He is our Father and Friend. Our praise is not mere exaltation. It is the praise of admiration, love, and devotion.

Praise ye the Lord!

How do we apply this Psalm to our lives?

This psalm requires us to treat God's name, His works, and His reputation carefully. This is the essence of the third commandment: "Ye shall not take the name of the Lord your God in vain." If we are to be prepared to praise God on Sundays, then we cannot be speaking of Him lightly and taking His name in vain the rest of the week. We must speak of our God with the utmost reverence and love throughout the day, every day.

How does this Psalm teach us to worship God?

Worship includes an exhortation to praise God. This entire psalm is a robust encouragement to everything and all people to praise God, for He is worthy to be worshiped. Throughout the service, we are given many reasons to worship God. Somewhere in the service, we must respond in praise. Some churches use a hymn of response after the sermon. This may be that point at which we lift our voices to praise God for His revelation of Himself. This is the obvious, logical conclusion to every message about God. Let us encourage one another to praise and worship!

Questions:

1. How does this psalm constitute a crescendo of praise? What sort of method is used to bring us all to praise?

2. How are the three sections ordered in this psalm? Who are we addressing in each section?

3. What is the highest creation of God?

4. How does this psalm present age-integrated, cross-generational worship?

5. What does God do for His people in the last verse?

Family Discussion Questions:

1. How do we express exaltation? What are the truths that encourage a spirit of exaltation in our praise?

2. What other created things would you call to the worship of God? Can you think of some amazing elements of the creation of God that you have learned about recently?

Psalm 149

Category: *Praise*
Occasion: *Tyrants Fall*
Author: *Unknown*

....

1 Praise ye the Lord. Sing unto the Lord a new song, and his praise in the congregation of saints.

2 Let Israel rejoice in him that made him: let the children of Zion be joyful in their King.

3 Let them praise his name in the dance: let them sing praises unto him with the timbrel and harp.

4 For the Lord taketh pleasure in his people: he will beautify the meek with salvation.

5 Let the saints be joyful in glory: let them sing aloud upon their beds.

6 Let the high praises of God be in their mouth, and a two-edged sword in their hand;

7 To execute vengeance upon the heathen, and punishments upon the people;

8 To bind their kings with chains, and their nobles with fetters of iron;

9 To execute upon them the judgment written: this honour have all his saints. Praise ye the Lord.

The Point:

When wicked tyrants come down, God's people rejoice and dance in praise before the true King.

How do we feel in the recitation of this Psalm?

The joy expressed in this psalm may come across as a little odd to those who have the modern conception of joy. The joy in this psalm is experienced when battles are won and the enemy is crushed. It is the joy of triumph that comes after military conquest. The most popular presidents are usually those who have won significant wars, men like George Washington or Abraham Lincoln. These earthly kings pale in comparison to our heavenly King and we ought to be a thousand times more thrilled when He rides into town.

What does this Psalm say?

Verses 1-5

How many love songs could a man write when he is enraptured with his espoused? God's people will instinctively express themselves in new songs of praise when their hearts are captured by love and devotion for God. This is the natural form of human expression that is built into a people who are created to glorify God. While many of the great hymns were written in times of the greatest Spirit-filled revivals in church history, we can only imagine the billions of new hymns of praise that will be written into eternity. Revived churches will be known by their new songs of praise put to new music, inspired by Spirit-filled hearts that love God, many of which have already been written. Some denominations only sing new songs outside of formal worship, and that is fine. The important thing is that the hearts of men rise up to praise God in spirit and in truth.

What a blessing to sing psalms and hymns in the congregation of the saints! We are called to a like-mindedness and unity, in order that we should "with one mind and one mouth glorify the God and Father of our Lord Jesus Christ" (Rom. 15:5, 6). This is the grand purpose of the church of Jesus Christ. This is the great end for which the church exists and will exist throughout eternity!

This praise, however, must not be confused with the praise of some terrible dictator of North Korea. These human tyrants require parades in their own honor every other week or so, where everybody dutifully shows up to parrot the mantras of praise. Should anybody be absent, they know they will be summarily executed for disloyalty. God's people, on the other hand, find great joy in this worship because they have a wholly different relationship with Him.

How? First, each member of Zion has been specially selected from all eternity to make up this body. Each has been redeemed, adopted into the family of God, and sanctified by the Holy Spirit of God. He has taken ugly sinners and made them beautiful saints. He has taken killers and cannibals and made them loving, gentle elders in His church. Moreover, our God genuinely takes pleasure in His people. He has been incredibly gracious to them, more than any King in the history of the world. And, He delights in them more than any earthly father delights in his little ones.

We are even to sing upon our beds. How often does this happen with any of us? Usually, our innermost thoughts surface when we are in the quiet of the bedroom. Here we are away from the hustle and the bustle of the day. If our thoughts are upon God's work in our lives, indeed we may burst forth in glorious praise as we lie in bed.

Dancing and musical instruments are added to the celebration in verse three. Some churches are not comfortable with adding these elements to their public worship services. Sincere Christians are always rightly concerned about promoting showmanship, shallow forms of amusement, or emotionalized and mindless worship in the church. When it comes to music, there are many traps to fall into, particularly in the day in which we live. Whether it occurs in formal worship or outside of it, there must be a role for instruments and dance for the saints. This psalm is speaking about praise music in the congregation (Verse. 1). The context for this psalm is important at this point: we are celebrating a victory over wicked powers, and the reign of our King. This is clearly a celebratory psalm, much like the psalm that Miriam sang when Pharaoh's hosts were decimated at the Red Sea. Churches that never quite resonate to this sentiment have not experienced the taste of victory, the sense of conquest, and the celebration that needs to attend the ascension of our King. This use of music and dance is most unfamiliar to the culture of the Western, secularized world.

Verses 6–9

The psalm takes an unusual turn in these last verses. We must remember that the kingly office of the Lord Jesus Christ has already been introduced in the second verse. Praise to God relates to various elements of His nature, persons, and offices. In this psalm, we specifically think of Jesus' kingly authority, His violence as He treads out the winepress of God's wrath against the nations, His spiritual conquests, and His rule over us.

We sing high praise as we realize Christ's kingly reign, but what about the second half of verse six? There is this two-edged sword in our hands with which we will execute vengeance upon the nations. What does this entail? The Christian life is portrayed as violent in many parts of the New Testament. The violent take the kingdom by force (Matt. 11:12). We tread upon Satan (Rom. 16:20). We cast down imaginations and every high thing that exalts itself above the knowledge of Christ (2 Cor. 10:5). We avenge disobedience (2 Cor. 10:6). Certainly, the risen Christ is bringing His enemies under His footstool (1 Cor. 15:25). Those kings and their empires that refuse to serve Christ always end up in the ash heap of history. But how are we involved in this binding of kings and taking vengeance on the heathen? We take the Gospel to the furthest ends of the earth. We are responsible for preaching the Word of God and wielding that mighty sword. We take down those imaginations that oppose Christ. The weapons of our warfare, however, are not carnal but mighty through God to the tearing down of strongholds (2 Cor. 10:4).

It may be hard to imagine this, but one day Hollywood's film industry, with all of its pride and lust that virtually dominates our culture, will be no more. The powerful, godless school systems that refuse to teach the fear of God as the very beginning of knowledge will be gone. Proud materialist states like the current Chinese communist government will be no more. The preaching of the Word of God and the prayers of the saints will avail much to destroy these enemies of Christ. Though the church's influence is practically imperceptible at times, and though the most uncompromising pastors are persecuted until there is hardly anything left of them, this fledgling church will end up treading on Satan. This is the modus operandi of our King. It is the foolishness of preaching that brings earthly kingdoms down. Christ will conquer through weakness, and He will never allow the enemy to win in the long run.

The world's power is already ruined by the cross. The Christian will say with the Apostle that this world has been crucified to me, and I to the world (Gal. 6:14). For the Christian, Jesus broke the world's back when He died on the cross. He told us, "In the world ye shall have tribulation: but be of good cheer; I have overcome the world" (Jn. 16:33). We are given the upper hand in these battles with the world, but the war continues until He returns to final and complete victory. PRAISE THE LORD!

How do we apply this Psalm to our lives?

Every part of this praise psalm applies to the Christian family. Singing in our beds, dancing before the Lord, playing our musical instruments—this should be the warp and woof of Christian family life. In no way should this be confined to a single meeting of the church on the first day of the week.

How does this Psalm teach us to worship God?

Our churches too often degrade into either an entertainment fest meant to amuse the crowds, or, a somber, subdued service that does not reflect the sentiment of victory we have in the Lord Jesus Christ. When will we find this loud celebration, dancing, and rejoicing rightly carried out? A right understanding of who God is, and what He has done for us through Jesus Christ, will yield the right kind of worship.

Questions:

1. What does this psalm say about writing new songs and new hymns of praise?

2. How does the worship of our King differ from the worship demanded by a human king or dictator?

3. How does the context of this psalm warrant dancing?

4. What is Jesus doing right now, as He sits on the right hand of the Father?

5. How do the saints bind kings with chains?

Family Discussion Questions:

1. Should dancing and musical instruments be brought into the church? How could we employ these means of praise in our family?

2. Do our gatherings err on one of these two sides: the "entertainment-fest" or the "somber, subdued service with no real sentiment for victory?" How might we adjust a bit?

PSALM 150

Category: *Praise*
Occasion: *Special Celebration of Praise*
Author: *Unknown*

....

1   Praise ye the Lord. Praise God in his sanctuary: praise him in the firmament of his power.
2   Praise him for his mighty acts: praise him according to his excellent greatness.
3   Praise him with the sound of the trumpet: praise him with the psaltery and harp.
4   Praise him with the timbrel and dance: praise him with stringed instruments and organs.
5   Praise him upon the loud cymbals: praise him upon the high sounding cymbals.
6   Let every thing that hath breath praise the Lord. Praise ye the Lord.

The Point:

This is a pure praise psalm, with no other purpose but to praise God with twelve phrases in six short verses.

How do we feel in the recitation of this Psalm?

We have reached a fitting end to the book of Psalms in this last psalm: with a crescendo of praise. The theme of this psalm increases in emphasis with each repetition, and we can hear the volume increasing with each of these twelve phrases of praise. Our hearts fill up with a holy pride, exaltation, glory, and delight over the God we worship. We desire to "make His praise glorious" through this great finale.

What does this Psalm say?

Verse 1

Twelve times, we cry out to ourselves and to anybody who may be in our vicinity: "Praise the Lord with me!" This repetition implies that there can never be an ending to the praise of the Lord our God. In John's revelation, we read of the four living creatures who never rest in their praise: "They rest not day and night, saying, Holy, holy, holy, Lord God Almighty, which was, and is, and is to come" (Rev. 4:8). This worship will continue into eternity because it is absolutely fitting, and a cessation of it would constitute the ultimate sacrilege. Thus, this psalm is a precursor to the heavenly and eternal praise we will witness at the final resurrection.

This verse introduces two contexts in which the praise takes place—in the "sanctuary" and the "firmament of His power." As we raise these praises, these settings are presented to our view. The sanctuary is the holy place where He dwells. In the Old Testament, it is the holiest of holies. In New Testament worship, it is the assembly of God's people where Christ is present.

"Having therefore, brethren, boldness to enter into the holiest by the blood of Jesus, by a new and living way, which he hath consecrated for us, through the veil, that is to say, his flesh; and having an high priest over the house of God; let us draw near with a true heart in full assurance of

faith, having our hearts sprinkled from an evil conscience, and our bodies washed with pure water." (Heb. 10:19-21)

The place itself renders a special awe in us, as we consider the precious, holy blood of Jesus that makes a way for sinners into the presence of God! We are overcome by the holiness of God in this place, but we are also overcome as we consider the expanse of His power. Here we have a view of the Lord's power as we rise up to look upon the created universe. The mere view of the earth from 25,000 feet in an airplane is enough to take your breath away. To see our sun as a tiny dot in the Milky Way galaxy is a billion times more impressive. Then, to consider that our galaxy is negligible in the scheme of the universe gives us something of a view of God's infinite power. Thus, our setting and view prepares us for the remainder of this mighty song of praise.

Verse 2

The second verse gives us more reason for praise. Our God has no need for mindless praise, so it is right that our minds be given some basis for worship. Therefore, in this particular psalm we are praising Him for 1.) His mighty acts, and 2.) His excellent greatness. Always, the reason for our praise and worship will be either based in God's nature or His works.

There is no ending to the study of God's wisdom and power in creation and providence. Man is incapable of understanding the basic building blocks of matter and life—the atom and the cell. We cannot plum the depths of His creation. We cannot reverse-engineer the complexities of life. If we cannot find the mighty works of God sufficient to drive us to our knees, we must be blinded by either gross ignorance or pride. But what about God's redemption and the mysteries of divine love? Even the angels have desired to look into the gloriousness of the incarnation, the sufferings of Christ, and the glory that followed (1 Pet. 1:12). If the angels are enthralled by this work of God, what shall our response be to it?

God is greater, in every respect, than everybody and everything else in existence. We cannot configure something greater than God. The cults that attempt it demonstrate the finitude and defectiveness of their systems. He is the great I AM, and He has never been and never will be the "I WILL BE" or "I WAS." His existence is absolute, eternal, and unchangeable. His attributes of power, wisdom, holiness, justice, goodness, and truth are infinite and absolute as well. There is no limitation or imperfection in God, in any respect. He is only prevented from limiting himself. He cannot succumb to imperfection. There is nothing more profound in the entire realm of reality than God Himself. Therefore, He is worthy of our study, our devotion, and our worship.

Verses 3–6

Having looked at the context and reason for this worship, the remainder of the psalm calls for praise using every mode of music available to man—musical instruments, vocals, and dance. The praise of God must be the primary use for music. Should music be used solely to glorify man and his interests, human culture will corrupt and degrade. This is the legacy of the popular music produced in the last two generations. The beginning of knowledge in the music classroom must be the fear of the Lord, and the worship of God must be the end of it.

Musical instruments accompany and evoke human emotions either rightly or wrongly, for a good cause or a bad cause. Music can makes us happy, sad, or excited. The highest purpose to which the human emotions of reverence, adoration, love, and rejoicing are employed must be in relationship to God our Creator and Redeemer. Therefore, music should be used to this end.

Music aids us in our worship, but true praise must begin in our hearts. We must first receive the good news, as we watch the Red Sea waters roll back on to the armies of Egypt. We must first thrill at the good news of the Gospel of Jesus Christ, that He has beaten sin and death at the cross. Then and only then, do we have reasons to celebrate. This special celebratory music demands the full accompaniment of trumpets, harps, timbrels, stringed instruments, organs, and cymbals. We call the whole orchestra to the purpose of praising God. There must be no question as to the purpose of the music. The words used in music should be understood by all, so that we do not miss the purpose for the music. We have no interest in humanist classical music played to the glory of man—none. We need everybody and every instrument praising the Lord in the hall.

Verse six includes the voices of every living person. This is not an instrumental piece. It is a choral number, and every person in the room is called to join in the choir, praising our God together.

PRAISE YE THE LORD!

How do we apply this Psalm to our lives?

- Instrumental music is part of Christian worship. Also, psalms, hymns, and spiritual songs must be a daily part of the Christian life, the Christian family, and the Christian home. While not everybody may be able to play a musical instrument, the Bible teaches that all should sing. We should therefore teach our children to sing, and it would be helpful if every home had some musical accompaniment. Practically every day, we should hear the psalms and hymns sung with gusto in the Christian home. This is just what Christians do (Eph. 5:19).

- Unless music is taught for the major purpose of worshiping God, our children will develop the wrong perspective of it. So much of music is wasted on the glory of man, on corrupting emotional allegiances, on immoral and worldly lusts, on vain and immature triteness, and on modern destructive ideas that advocate chaos, meaninglessness, and nihilism. Music programs in modern colleges are extremely dangerous in that they do not teach the beginning of knowledge as the fear of God. These humanist systems are sure to fail, because they do not worship God "in His sanctuary and in the firmament of His power."

How does this Psalm teach us to worship God?

The business of the Christian church is actually very simple. We come into worship first to be reminded of more reasons to praise God, and then we praise Him. As we enter worship on a Sunday morning, we lean forward, asking, as it were, "Would you give me another reason to worship God?" Sometimes we find new reasons, and sometimes we hone old reasons by clarifying our understanding of God's creation and His redemption.

There are times in which we must focus upon worshiping God, and nothing else. This psalm may be used to that end. As we sing this psalm, we dedicate ourselves fully to God's praise and worship. Our greatest crescendos, our greatest joy, and our greatest experiences in worship occur when our hearts rise to this praise for our God.

Questions:

1. How many times do we "praise the Lord" in this psalm?

2. What are the two contexts from which we issue our praise (in verse 1)?

3. What are the two things about God for which we praise Him (in verse 2)?

4. What are the modes by which we are encouraged to praise the Lord in the last verses of the psalm?

5. How can music be used for good or for evil? What is the highest good for which we may employ our music?

Family Discussion Questions:

1. How have we used music in our family? Have we viewed music primarily as a means by which we praise the Lord and thank the Lord?

2. Where does true praise begin for you? What are the works of God, or the teachings from Scripture, that are most inspirational in helping you to praise?

APPENDIX: CATEGORY & OCCASION

Psalm	*Category*	*Occasion*
120	Ascent, Deliverance	Ungodly company
121	Ascent, Faith	Threats to Safety
122	Ascent, Thanksgiving	Sunday Morning
123	Ascent, Deliverance	Corporate Affliction
124	Ascent, Faith	Narrow Escape
125	Ascent, Faith	Rise in Tyranny
126	Ascent, Thanksgiving	Church Restoration
127	Ascent, Faith	Building a Home
128	Ascent, Faith	The Blessed Life
129	Imprecatory, Ascent	Enemies Hating the Church
130	Faith, Ascent	Long Term Isolation/Imprisonment
131	Faith, Ascent	Humbled
132	Didactic, Ascent	Church in Disarray
133	Didactic	Healthy Ecumenical Meetings
134	Ascent, Praise	A Short Church Service
135	Praise	Casting Down Idols
136	Thanksgiving	Remembrance of God's Temporal and Eternal Blessings
137	Imprecatory	A Decimated Church
138	Praise	Trouble on Every Side
139	Confession, Imprecatory	Meditation on God's Presence
140	Deliverance, Imprecatory	Spiritual Assaults
141	Deliverance	Self-doubt
142	Deliverance	Abandoned, Isolated, and Persecuted
143	Deliverance	Hard Persecution
144	Faith	Worldly Corruption
145	Praise	Remembering the Goodness of God
146	Praise	Political Elections

Psalm	*Category*	*Occasion*
147	Praise	Viewing Nature
148	Praise	Age-integrated Worship
149	Praise	Tyrants Fall
150	Praise	Special Celebration of Praise

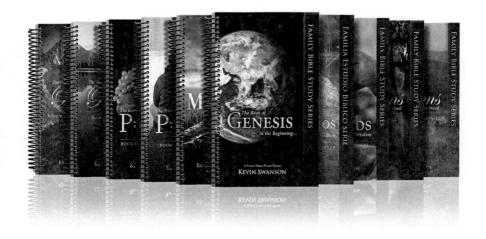

To order other Family Bible Study Guides, go to www.generations.org, call 888-389-9080, or send an e-mail to mail@generations.org

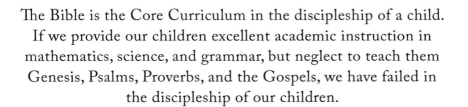

The Bible is the Core Curriculum in the discipleship of a child. If we provide our children excellent academic instruction in mathematics, science, and grammar, but neglect to teach them Genesis, Psalms, Proverbs, and the Gospels, we have failed in the discipleship of our children.